THE OFFICIAL AUTHORIZED STORY OF DESMOND DOSS
(ABRIDGED VERSION)

✝
HERO OF
HACKSAW

THE GRIPPING TRUE STORY THAT INSPIRED THE MOVIE

RIDGE

BOOTON HERNDON

POSTSCRIPT BY
DOUG BATCHELOR

Published by
Remnant Publications, Inc.
649 E. Chicago Rd.
Coldwater, MI 49036

Cover Design by David Berthiaume
Layout and design by Greg Solie • Altamont Graphics

ISBN: 978-1-629131-54-2

TABLE OF CONTENTS

CHAPTER 1

THE LONELIEST SOLDIER

Time for the welcome sound of taps drew nearer, and a hubbub of noise and confusion filled the long wooden barracks as the men of Company D prepared to hit the sack. It had been an exhausting, exasperating day. The famous old World War I division, the 77th, had been reactivated to serve in another war, and training was just beginning. The division's insignia, the Statue of Liberty, indicated its headquarters, and the men assigned to it were typical of the melting pot of New York City. Many had been scooped up by the draft in the winter and spring of 1942, just after Pearl Harbor, and were older, tougher, and more cynical than the usual crop of draftees. Now, milling about the plain wooden barracks in various stages of undress—green fatigues, olive drab underwear—they were protesting loudly and obscenely in the harsh accent of the big city against everything and everybody.

In the midst of the racket a slender young man with wavy brown hair sat quietly on his neatly made, brown-blanketed bed. If the day had been a rough one for the older, tougher men, for him it had been a nightmare. He had come into the Army willingly, but as a conscientious objector, a noncombatant. Though eager to serve his country, he had the written assurance of the President of the United States Franklin D. Roosevelt through Executive Order Number 8606 and the Chief of Staff of the Army that he would not have to bear arms. He had naturally assumed that he would be assigned to some phase of medical training. Now here he was in an infantry company. A little on the gawky side, with the flat drawl of the Southern mountains, he neither looked nor sounded like the rest of the men in the barracks.

Not just for solace, but as an integral and meaningful part of his daily life, the young soldier had turned to his Bible. As always he found in it, in the Word of God, a feeling of comfort and peace. He closed the Book and, in a natural motion developed over many years, slipped to his knees at the side of his bunk to say his prayers.

"Hey, look at the preacher!" somebody shouted above the racket. "He's prayin'!"

Howls of derision, hoots, and catcalls sounded through the barracks. The young soldier continued his prayers, motionless on his knees.

The big-city men, irritable and keyed-up after a day of strain and tension in a new, demanding environment, were ready to relieve their emotions on any scapegoat, and now they had found one. A heavy Army shoe sailed over a bunk and clunked on the floor beside the pious young rookie. It was a near miss. Another shoe came flying and another, accompanied by more profane remarks. The man on his knees, though frightened and confused, remained where he was. He didn't want to get hit with a shoe, but he didn't want to cut his prayers short either. This was no time to offend the Lord!

From outside came the sound of the first notes of taps. The sergeant in charge of the barracks stuck his head into the long room and hollered, "Hey, you guys, settle down in there!"

The lights went out. The barracks quieted down. The young soldier, his prayers finished, crawled beneath the covers. As the clear, mournful notes of taps faded in the spring night, he lay silently in the hard, narrow bunk, his eyes glistening with tears of loneliness and pain.

So ended the first day of Private Desmond T. Doss in the 77th Infantry Division.

The days immediately following proved no better than the first. At night, in the barracks, the ridicule continued. Though he now waited for lights out before kneeling to say his prayers, still an occasional shoe hurtled through the darkness in his direction. What hurt more than anything else was hearing the third commandment being shattered all around him. The men learned that calling him "holy Jesus" caused him great distress. One tough-voiced, hard-drinking man in his thirties named Karger,[1] who seemed to hate everybody and everything including religion, went out of his way to taunt Doss in his harsh voice. Desmond would cringe. He had never in his life heard anyone take the name of the Lord in vain so brazenly.

---

1   All the names in this book are real except for three: Karger, Steinman, and Cosner. Mr. Doss has asked that their real identity be concealed in order to avoid embarrassing them at this late date.

Karger apparently enjoyed taking his perpetual foul humor out on Desmond. "When we go into combat, Doss," he would say, "you're not comin' back alive. I'm gonna shoot you myself." Then he'd laugh.

By day the noncombatant had another problem. Though assigned to the infantry, he would not accept a weapon. In vain did the supply sergeant, the platoon sergeant, the lieutenant commanding the platoon, and the captain commanding the company, order him to take a gun. The slender private respectfully refused to do so. He was alternately threatened, shouted at, pleaded with, and coaxed.

He appreciated the position of his superior officers, and he didn't want to cause anybody trouble. It was simply that he had received a prior order from a Higher Authority.

Religion was to Desmond Doss a direct and a personal thing. He had been raised in a Seventh-day Adventist home, had received his entire formal education in a one-room Seventh-day Adventist school, and had been active—fully, intensely, and exclusively—in a Seventh-day Adventist church. His mother, his teachers, and his church leaders had taught him that the Holy Bible is the Word of God, and Desmond had accepted their teachings completely. He did not consider the Ten Commandments as mere guides to conduct, to be followed when possible. To him they were, rather, just what the Holy Bible declares them to be: The will of the Lord God Almighty. Desmond believed that they applied to him, Desmond Thomas Doss, personally and directly.

On the wall of the living room, back in the little frame house in Lynchburg, Virginia, hung a framed scroll depicting the Ten Commandments. Often as a little boy Desmond had pushed a chair over to the wall and climbed up on it in order to study the painting more closely. These periods of religious art study would take place only when his parents weren't home, incidentally; there was a family commandment which expressly forbade children to stand on living-room chairs.

Each commandment was illustrated by a drawing. The one that gripped Desmond most concerned the sixth commandment: *Thou shalt not kill.* It depicted the story of Cain and Abel. In the illustration Abel lay on the ground bleeding, while over him stood the murderous Cain, dagger in hand.

Little Desmond would stare at that picture in horror and fascination. How could a man be so evil as to slay his own brother? Desmond himself belonged to a warm, loving, happy family. His father, William Thomas Doss, was a carpenter who, during Desmond's childhood, provided a comfortable living for his wife and three children. Desmond, born in February 1919, was the middle child. His sister Audrey was four years older; his brother, Harold Edward, two years younger.

One time when Harold came down with a rare type of influenza that brought on a high fever, the rest of the family sat up all night with him. He was delirious and in such agony that at one point his mother fell to her knees beside his bed and prayed. As Desmond remembered it, she repeated the words from the Lord's prayer, "Thy will be done," and then continued: "And if it be Thy will, oh, Lord, to take Harold, please do it now. Please let him be laid to rest and not suffer any longer. But if it is not Thy will to take him, please spare him this pain. We ask it in Jesus' name."

Soon after that prayer the fever broke, and Harold's pain and delirium subsided into a deep sleep. The next morning, the doctor was amazed at his recovery. Mrs. Doss told him how she had prayed. The doctor nodded with understanding. "Son," he told Harold, "the Lord has spared you."

To young Desmond, brothers were to be prayed for. Standing on a chair in the living room, studying the illustration of Cain killing his brother, Desmond knew that he would obey the sixth commandment and *all* commandments as long as he lived.

Baseball was the most popular sport in Lynchburg during Desmond's childhood. The kids began tossing balls back and forth on the first sunny day of early spring, and continued playing all summer long. Desmond enjoyed playing as much as anyone else until the day, when he was eight years old, he fell and cut his hand on a broken bottle. The jagged glass sliced through several tendons, all across the palm of his hand.

The family doctor looked at it, tested the dangling fingers, and shook his head sadly. "You'll never be able to use this hand again, Desmond," he said.

Desmond's mother did not give up so easily. When the cut was healed, she began massaging his injured hand, moving his fingers. With her help and encouragement he regained the use of his fingers. But the scar, which ran completely across the palm, remained sensitive. He could no longer participate in any sport requiring two good hands.

At first young Desmond was crushed. But as the days went on, he found there were other things a high-spirited youngster could do besides play games. Rather than sit and mope around the house, he did more than his share of the household chores. His mother loved flowers, and he would work with her by the hour, helping her and nature create beauty. They had so many flowers that they began sharing them with others less fortunate. At first they gave flowers to their neighbors, especially when someone happened to be sick. People were so appreciative that Desmond also began taking flowers to the hospital and even to the city jail. Sharing beauty, he discovered, was even better than raising it.

The visits were not always pleasant. One patient—an indigent, aged man with no friends or relatives left in the world—was dying with an incurable disease. He could not afford a nurse, and Desmond volunteered to stay with him. The pain the poor old man suffered was so intense that Desmond could almost feel the hurt himself. He couldn't stand it and ran out to get the doctor.

"Please give him something for the pain!" the boy pleaded.

The doctor patted him on the shoulder. "I've already given him a massive dose," he said. "I can't give him any more."

That night death spared the patient further misery. Desmond went home, but he could not sleep. He could still hear those cries and groans of pain. However, the boy did not regret having been at the old man's bedside. He had done what he could; the patient had not died alone and friendless.

The boy had learned that even in such an unhappy situation there can be a positive feeling of satisfaction from having done the best he could to help a fellow human being. This was in itself a reward.

But sometimes more positive good resulted. One Sabbath, church services were interrupted for an announcement that a woman, a former member, was in desperate need of a blood transfusion. Desmond, along with several members of the congregation, hurried to the hospital. No one mentioned the fact that neither the woman nor her husband attended the church. They were Adventists, but there had been some misunderstanding when they moved to Lynchburg some time before. They thought they were not welcome at the church, and then it became a matter of pride to stay away.

It was Desmond's blood, and his only, which matched that of the ill woman. He was only a skinny boy in his early teens, but the patient's condition was critical, and he offered his blood without hesitation. After giving it, he got off the table on which he had been lying and had to grab a hatrack to keep from falling to the floor.

The woman pulled through. She and her husband asked Desmond to come see them. They offered first to pay him, then, when he refused, asked if they could not give him some kind of present.

"Yes, you can give me a present," the boy said. "Come to church."

They did, and became active, dedicated members of the congregation.

With this background, Desmond Doss was poured into the mold of the model medical soldier of the United States Army. The higher echelons of the military establishment in Washington were fully aware of the existence of men like Doss and had established an official policy to use them. A quarter of a century before, in World War I, bona fide conscientious objectors had been mistreated and imprisoned. Men were kicked, beaten, and dunked headfirst into latrines. During the war, 162 members of the Seventh-day Adventist Church alone were court-martialed because of their religious convictions, and when the war ended thirty-five of these men were serving terms of from five to twenty years at hard labor. Thanks to tireless efforts on the part of religious leaders, and to the American tradition of religious freedom, all of these men were given full pardons on Armistice Day, 1918.

In the period between wars interest increased in the question of how the young Adventist could serve his country, as he is specifically adjured to do in Romans 13:1, and yet obey the sixth commandment. An elaborate program developed in which the church and the armed services cooperated to enable Adventists to serve where they were best suited, in the medical department. In 1934 the Adventists organized a Medical Cadet Corps to train their youth of preservice age in the fundamentals of military medical service. Several Adventist colleges and academies in the United States and other countries set up MCC units. The accent was on service to the nation within the framework of religious belief. In recognition of the valuable service which can be rendered by young men eager to serve their country, but without taking human life, the Congress of the United States specifically wrote into the military draft law the provision that conscientious objectors be assigned to the medical department.

Desmond Doss was fully aware of the situation. He registered for the draft along with the other young men of Lynchburg, and was classified

I-A-O. The "O" stood for "conscientious objector," and Desmond put in a mild protest to his draft board about it.

"I'm not a conscientious objector," he said. "I'm willing to serve. What I am is a noncombatant."

"There isn't any such classification," he was told. "You're in I-A-O and that's where you're going to stay."

According to the official procedure worked out by the church and the armed services, Adventists would not volunteer for service, but would wait their turn in the draft. While waiting, Desmond had worked in a shipyard, a vital war industry, and had taken a course in first aid to prepare himself for service when the call came. When it did come, a shipyard official suggested to him that he could seek deferment on the grounds of being essential to industry. He refused even to consider it.

"I'm not essential here, and you know it," he said.

Many of Desmond's friends enlisted. Several were classified 4-F, unfit for military service. There were those who took their own lives out of disappointment and embarrassment of not being able to serve their country. Desmond was profoundly affected. Despite his mother's pleadings, and his father's objections, Desmond, desperately wanting to do his patriotic duty enlisted in the Army and entered military service April 1, 1942, at Camp Lee, Virginia. Instead of being sent to basic training in the medical department, however, he found himself with the newly reactivated 77th Division at Fort Jackson, South Carolina. The men were to train as a unit. In the confusion of those early days, Desmond Doss, draft classification I-A-O, was stuck in a rifle company.

There is a saying in the Army, whenever anybody complains—"Go tell it to the chaplain." That is exactly what Doss did. The chaplain, Captain Carl Stanley, received him warmly and listened to his story. Captain Stanley had a close friend in the ministry of the Seventh-day Adventist Church, and he was well acquainted with the customs and beliefs of this comparatively small, but extremely active, Protestant denomination. He knew that this soldier was a bona fide objector and as such entitled by law to be assigned to the medical department. Captain Stanley explained the situation at division headquarters. Desmond was placed in the medics where he belonged and began his training as a medical soldier.

Military medicine is a kind of advanced first aid, applicable to the battlefield. Desmond learned the contents of his two large canvas first-aid kits, and the specific use of each item. There were the battle dressings of various sizes to be placed over open wounds. There were packages of sulfanilamide powder to be sprinkled over open wounds before the dressing was put in place. There were syrettes of morphine to be injected to alleviate the pain. Desmond learned not only how to make the injection, but, of equal importance, when to use the drug and when not. In some types of wounds morphine can be fatal.

With the other rookie medics, he learned how to use whatever material was at hand—saplings, rifle stocks—to make splints for broken limbs. He learned how to give blood plasma on the battlefield, what to do for shock, when to administer water and when to withhold it. It was like going to school again. Desmond remembered the little brown-shingled school operated by the church back in Lynchburg. There was only one teacher for eight grades, but each grade contained only a few children. The teacher would work with each class in turn.

Desmond had been unable to continue school after the eighth grade. The depression that came in with the thirties made it difficult for his father to obtain work, and Desmond had to pitch in to help support the family. He found a job in a lumberyard doing rough, heavy work for ten cents an hour, fifty hours a week. Of that five dollars he gave fifty cents to the church as his tithe and $3 to his mother. He spent 50 cents a week for carfare and with the remaining dollar bought all of his clothing and necessities.

Though regular school was over for him, he continued to go to Sabbath School. On the wall of the Sabbath School room hung a large picture of the Sea of Galilee. Each pupil could place on it little boat-like stickers for being present and on time, knowing the lesson, and knowing the memory verse. For an additional incentive, if you could say all of the memory verses for an entire three months, you would get a Bible. For each quarter of perfect attendance the award was a bookmark. When he was just a youngster, Desmond missed one session, and that wiped out his attendance record for the entire quarter. From then on he never missed, nor did he ever fail to prepare his lesson.

One day the family visited relatives out of town and didn't get back until late at night. The next day was the Sabbath, and Desmond had not prepared his lesson. Though he was so tired and sleepy he could barely make out the words, he still stayed up and completed the assignment. In the morning he dragged his weary body out of bed and to Sabbath School.

He had worked too many hours preparing his lessons over the preceding part of the year, had unfailingly attended too many Sabbath School sessions, to permit one lapse to cost him the benefits and rewards of perfect attendance. He was protecting his investment of time and study.

In this way, to Desmond Doss, conscientious attention to duty became a way of life. Sometimes, at Fort Jackson, in an afternoon class on a hot day following a morning of vigorous exercise and a heavy midday dinner, with an instructor droning away on how to purify water or how flies can carry disease, some of the men would start to nod. Not Desmond. He was there, he stayed awake, and he listened. It was his way of life.

Would you not believe, then, that this earnest, attentive medical soldier would have earned the respect and admiration of his officers, if not his fellow recruits? Instead, he was considered an oddball, a headache, a troublemaker by his officers, even up to the headquarters of the regiment.

Why were they down on him when he tried to be an exemplary soldier, a "conscientious cooperator" rather than an objector, in everything his religion did not forbid?

There were several strikes against him. Prejudice against conscientious objectors prevailed, and although Desmond hated to admit it, he could see why. There were three other "conchies" in the division, and Desmond had no use for any of them. He was eager to serve his country in a noncombatant capacity, but these three guys wanted no part of military life, period. Their only dedication was to the avoidance of work. And one of them, whose teeth were black from snuff, was downright repulsive. One day they were no longer with the division, for which everyone was thankful, but in the meantime, Desmond suffered through association.

"You guys are all alike," one of his sergeants accused him. "You talk big about religious freedom, but when your country needs you to help protect that freedom you chicken out."

"That's where you're wrong, sergeant," Desmond said earnestly. "In my church we're taught to obey government authority, just like the Bible says. You'll never find me failing to salute the flag or trying to get out of a detail. I love this country just as much as you do."

Sometimes when the infantry marched out to the rifle range to spend the day in marksmanship training, Desmond would go along. But of course he would not participate. The hot, hard-working riflemen down on the shooting line, blasting off round after round until their ears rang and their shoulders ached, saw their medic standing around doing nothing, and naturally they resented him.

But the main reason for Desmond's unpopularity was his insistence on keeping the fourth commandment.

"Remember the Sabbath day, to keep it holy," the Lord told Moses some 3,500 years ago, and Desmond, as we have seen, heeded the Word of God as he understood it. Those words applied to the human race in general and to him, Desmond Doss, in particular. No one—neither the commander of the battalion, the regiment, or the division, nor the President of the United States—could make Desmond Doss disobey a commandment given him by God. The only exception to the fourth commandment was that put forward by the Son of God, Jesus Christ. Desmond's Bible had told him that Christ had healed the sick on the Sabbath. Desmond was also more than willing on the Sabbath to help sick people and, in combat, the wounded.

But there in South Carolina, thousands of miles from the fighting front, the sick were taken to the hospital and there were no wounded. Desmond could see no conceivable reason for disobeying the fourth commandment.

What made life especially difficult there in the 77th Division was the fact that Desmond, as a Seventh-day Adventist, did not observe Sunday, the first day of the week, but Saturday, the seventh. *Six days shalt thou labor, and do all thy work: but the seventh day is the Sabbath of the Lord thy God: in it thou shalt not do any work.* Desmond had known these words by heart almost as long as he could remember.

The 77th Division, of course, and the rest of the Armed Forces, recognized Sunday both as a day of rest and a day of worship. Practically all activities at Fort Jackson terminated Saturday afternoon and were not resumed until Monday morning. There was a chapel on the post with services for both Catholics and Protestants. Every large unit had its own chaplain who could hold services right there. Maneuvers were usually scheduled to terminate before Sunday, but if they did continue through the weekend, provision was made to hold Sunday services in the field.

As a seventh-day observer in a first-day Army, therefore, Desmond found himself doubly out of step. First, his religion forbade him to work from sundown Friday until sundown Saturday, which necessitated being officially excused from every operation during that period, every week. And second, because there were no Christian services held on the post on Saturday, he had to secure a pass to go into town to attend services there.

These services usually included a young people's meeting Friday night and regular church services Saturday morning.

It quickly became evident that in the matter of the United States Army versus Private Desmond T. Doss over the issue of the Sabbath, one of the two must back down, and it would not be Desmond. His first altercation over this matter occurred on his second day in the Army. He was inducted on a Friday. Saturday morning the sergeant ordered everybody to start scrubbing the barracks floor for Saturday inspection. Desmond refused to participate. He had come into the Army prepared to perform necessary duties on the Sabbath, as he believed Christ had done. But scrubbing the floor was not, in his mind, a necessary duty. A floor can be scrubbed any day in the week. It was certainly not going to be scrubbed the next day, Sunday.

The sergeant called in the lieutenant. The lieutenant couldn't get anywhere with the stubborn Sabbath keeper either, and angrily told him to get out of the barracks. Doss stepped outside, but a major came along and ordered him back in. He spent his first Sabbath in the Army huddled in a corner of the barracks while the other men, working, invented nasty remarks and passed them along to him gratis.

It was the same thing all over again when he joined the 77th Division. On his first Friday he consulted the chaplain about getting a pass to go into Columbia to church. The chaplain, Captain Stanley, pointed out that regulations prohibited giving any man a pass for any reason during his first two weeks in the camp.

"I believe that God will work out a way for me to go to church," Private Doss told the chaplain.

Captain Stanley sighed. He knew those Seventh-day Adventists. "I'll see what I can do at division headquarters," he said. That afternoon the pass came through.

By the next week Desmond had been transferred from the rifle company to the medical battalion. He reported to the battalion CO, Major Fred Steinman,[2] to ask for a pass to go to church on Saturday. The major's concern was with the training of a battalion. He gave Desmond his pass, but when he continued to come back week after week, the officer became annoyed. "This is the last one," he warned one Friday. "Don't come back for any more."

---

2   A pseudonym.

Desmond knew the major meant it. He asked the people in church next day to pray for him. And on the following Friday he asked for another pass. The major blew up and told him to get out. Again Desmond went to Captain Stanley. The chaplain took the matter up with division headquarters and it was determined that the Adventist soldier would have his Saturdays off just as the other men had their Sundays. Desmond had won except that in the Army it is not wise for privates to win over majors.

In actuality Desmond was never any better off than anybody else. In exchange for his Saturdays off, he pulled special duty on Sunday, all day Sunday. But none of the other men were around to see him that day and resented his Saturday freedom just the same. "You get more passes than the general," they complained.

The reaction among the infantrymen was especially bitter. There were the differences in speech and habits, his idleness at the rifle range, and now this special privilege. News of the strange soldier spread throughout the regiment. One day Desmond ran into Karger, that hard, cynical older man in Company D who had taken such delight in tormenting him before.

"You think you're so holy, Doss," Karger told him, adding some expletives. "Well, when we get in combat I'm gonna shoot you down like a dog."

It's not easy to live with men who hate you, especially when your sole mission is learning to care for those very men. This was a lonely, frustrating period for Private Doss.

At such a time a man turns not to his mother, not to his minister, not to the chaplain. He tells his troubles to his girl.

Desmond's girl was pretty, blond, serious, and, like him, a devout Seventh-day Adventist. Her name was Dorothy Schutte, and she was from Richmond, Virginia. She was one of seven children of a disabled veteran of World War I, and the family barely got by on his pension. Dorothy had determined to make something of her life. The first thing she must do, she realized, was get an education. That required money. When she was still in high school she got a job as a colporteur, selling Adventist books. Desmond met her when she came through Lynchburg. He and his family extended a normal amount of southern—plus Adventist—hospitality; they took her for a drive one Sabbath afternoon.

That fall Dorothy attended Washington Missionary College in Washington, D.C. She supported herself by working as a domestic in the home of a Washington family. Her work kept her from carrying a full scholastic schedule, but she didn't complain. She was on her way.

Adventists form a close group, something like a large family, and it was perfectly natural for Desmond to keep hearing of this ambitious young woman who was determined to get an education. She was the kind of girl he would like to know better.

Desmond had never had a sweetheart. He had gone around with groups of young Adventists, but had never become interested in one girl. He had made up his mind to save his love and his affection for the girl he would marry. He was twenty-two years old before he gathered up his courage and sought his first date. Before his induction he was working in a shipyard in Newport News, Virginia, for one dollar an hour; he had a secondhand car; he was rich. One Saturday morning he drove the 200 miles to Washington hoping to see Dorothy Schutte.

People were just beginning to enter Columbia Hall, the college chapel, for Sabbath services when he arrived. He looked for her but didn't see her. Finally services began, and he went on into the chapel and took a seat. There, right in front of him, sat Dorothy! He leaned forward and whispered Hello, but she shushed him without turning around. He had driven 200 miles for a "Sh-h-h!"

After the services, the congregation gathered in groups outside to talk. Dorothy was standing with a young married couple she knew. Desmond joined her just as they were inviting her to dinner.

"She's having dinner with me!" Desmond blurted.

Dorothy shot him a quick look, but she did not correct him. They did have dinner together, and all that afternoon, and supper too.

Desmond was well known as one of the young lay leaders of the church. He and Dorothy had several interests in common, and a great many mutual friends, and the conversation never flagged. He had intended to go on back to Newport News that day, but he put that thought out of his mind. He had found her now. He stayed over and spent Sunday with her, too, until it was time for her to prepare her lessons. For once Desmond disapproved of conscientiousness. But Dorothy said she would be happy to see him again, and Desmond sang all the way back to Newport News.

From then on, Desmond drove to Washington every other weekend. Several visits later, he and Dorothy double-dated with another Adventist couple. Desmond and Dorothy were in the back seat, and, driving through

Rock Creek Park, he kissed her. He was lucky she didn't knock his head off, because she was furious. Her face turned a flaming red. She had never been kissed before. Like Desmond, she was saving her love and affection for the person she would marry.

Desmond saw the look on her face. "I love you," he said quickly. It was the first time he had said those words. That made the kiss all right. For, Dorothy confessed, she loved him too.

But he was in no position to propose. They had discussed wartime marriages, and both opposed them. Desmond knew he would be called into service any day. When the notice came from the draft board, he made the last visit to Washington to see her.

"Will you wait for me?" he asked.

"Yes, I will," she said. Those were the most wonderful words he had ever heard.

They spent the rest of Desmond's last date with her as a civilian talking about the life they would lead after the war. It was amazing how similar their dreams were. Neither wanted a big house, or riches. They would both be satisfied with the most humble home as long as it was a Christian home. They resolved to have family worship every morning and every night. They both wanted lots of children to love and to bring up in the Christian faith.

They parted tearfully but bravely. Both felt sure they were doing the right thing.

As the lonely weeks at Fort Jackson went by, as Desmond found his misery increasing, the letters from Dorothy became more and more important. They encouraged him to keep going. Her love for him was the sole comfort in his friendless existence. He asked her to come to Columbia on a weekend, and she did, staying with an Adventist family he had met at church. They spent a warm and happy Sabbath together. This time the leave-taking was not so easy.

On the long Fourth of July weekend Desmond took the long bus ride to Richmond to surprise her. When he arrived, he learned that she had gone to Columbia to surprise him. They could continue to cross paths for days, so Desmond stayed put. Dorothy meanwhile had learned that he had gone to Richmond, and caught the next train back. They still had two days together.

Gradually Dorothy and Desmond realized that they did not want to wait until after the war was over. Both discussed their problems with their ministers, and they were advised to do what they thought best. That was the answer they wanted, for what they thought best was to be together, as man and wife, every possible minute. Dorothy and her mother began arranging for a wedding at their church.

But Desmond's commanding officers had no intention of letting this Seventh-day troublemaker go off and get married. No one would give him a definite answer to his request for a furlough. In desperation Desmond went over the head of the battalion commander, to the regimental adjutant. He was waiting there when in came the commander of the regiment, Colonel William H. Craig, the silver eagles of his rank gleaming. He was the highest-ranking officer Desmond had ever seen, and the most formidable.

"Is there anything I can do for you, soldier?" the colonel asked.

"If anybody can, you can," Desmond said, quickly adding, "Sir! I want to get married!"

The colonel listened to Desmond's story and apparently decided that he was sincere. He picked up the telephone and called the medical battalion.

"Why can't this man get married?" the colonel demanded. "When a man makes up his mind to get married you might as well let him go!"

Desmond was given his furlough. He and Dorothy were married in a quiet ceremony in Dorothy's church. She came back with him to Fort Jackson. Just knowing she was nearby made military life easier to bear.

CHAPTER 2

"...THAT YE MAY BE ABLE TO BEAR IT"

Reveille sounded with a strident urgency one Tuesday morning in late summer. "Come on," roared the sergeants, "get out of those sacks. Today's the day!"

"You don't have to rub it in, Sarge," one of the men in B Company groaned.

They had known it was coming for days. Now it was here. The company was moving out, right after chow, on its first long march. *Twenty-five miles,* with full field pack and a rifle. The march would be completed in eight hours; that meant an average of better than three miles an hour. This was the day that would separate the men from the boys.

"Hey, here's the preacher," one of the riflemen called out as Doss took his place with the 2d Platoon. "How come you didn't get a pass to go to church today?"

"Aw, what's he got to worry about?" another man growled. "No rifle, no ammunition, he's got it made in the shade."

The silent medic grinned, but didn't bother to reply. The two canvas first-aid kits he was carrying were almost as heavy as a rifle and twice as awkward. But he had a feeling he'd be needing the kits before the day was out.

This was more than a physical test for Desmond. It was his first real operation with the men with whom he would go into combat. He was now officially designated as a company aid man, one of the three medical soldiers, or medics, assigned to an infantry company.

For administrative purposes he came under the direction of the medical battalion of the 307th Regiment, but it was the riflemen, the doughboys, the dogfaces, of the 2d Platoon, Company B, 1st Battalion, 307th Infantry, thirty-eight men and one officer, with whom he would go into combat. They would be his medical charges. He would be expected to go to them, even at the risk of his own neck, if they needed him. They should share a close and mutual relationship, he and the men of the 2d Platoon, but in those first days it was just the other way around.

As had been the case with the first company to which he was assigned, the men of Company B were mostly from New York; nearly all were from the North. They were older and tougher, and exuded profanity. They had never known anyone like the soft-voiced young Southerner with his ever-present Bible. They called him "the preacher." They teased him about being married and insisted on dragging Dorothy's name into their earthy remarks about sex. This offended him deeply. He loved Dorothy and knew her to be a Christian woman with high ideals. Their marriage was blessed by God.

The two officers in B Company with whom Doss had contact were Captain Frank L. Vernon, the company commander, and Lieutenant Cecil L. Gornto, 2d Platoon leader. Captain Vernon, a fair and square South Carolinian who gave all he had to the task at hand and expected his men to do likewise, had no time for spare wheels like company aid men. Lieutenant Gornto, an articulate Floridian, was too busy striving to get his platoon up to the high standard of the CO, Captain Vernon, to worry about one medic.

The first sergeant called the company to attention, and turned it over to Captain Vernon. "All right, men," the captain said, in his positive, determined voice, "we've all been training for this for weeks. I expect every man to give it all he's got, and finish this hike on his feet! Platoon leaders, take command of your platoons!"

Lieutenant Gornto, at his place at the head of the 2d Platoon, whipped his hand up to his helmet in a snappy salute. Captain Vernon sang out the orders, the platoon leaders echoing, and B Company swung out of the company area, counting cadence at the top of its collective voice.

Even in the early morning, the summer sun shone hot in the South Carolina sky. The atmosphere was humid. By the time the company had crossed over the first of the rugged little sandy hills, their green cotton fatigues were splotched with sweat. The heat of the day was yet to come and twenty-four miles still lay ahead of them.

By midday the sun beat down like a big broiler in the sky. Some of the men had already drunk a full canteen of water, and now they had no more. They staggered like zombies, their eyes pulled back in red, sweating faces. Suddenly one of the men slumped to his knees and collapsed. Doss hurried to him. It was one of the older fellows, a man in his late thirties. His skin was clammy, his pulse barely perceptible. It was a clear-cut case of heat prostration. Desmond made him as comfortable as possible and turned him over to the ambulance that followed. Then he had to run to catch up with the company.

Captain Vernon, as fresh and tough as he had been when he started, was furious with the soldier for dropping out, and with Doss for not managing somehow to keep him on his feet.

At high noon they took a lunch break—K rations. Desmond had hardly choked down a mouthful when a soldier, slumped under a small tree, called him. The man had his shoe off and was examining a large blister on his heel.

"Can you do anything for this?" he asked.

"I'll sure try," Desmond said. He pricked the blister with a sterile needle, painted it with merthiolate, and then covered it tightly with a gauze dressing. Before he had finished, another man called him. Another, and another, all with the same ailment. While the men of Company B sprawled on their backs, Doss was busy fixing feet. For some severe cases he fashioned a doughnut-shaped pad to relieve the pressure.

It seemed they had been resting only a minute when the first sergeant blew his whistle. "Fall in," he shouted. "It's a long way back."

Blisters and sore feet kept Desmond busy all the way back. He'd fix up a man as best he could, then run to catch up with his platoon. Some of the men he treated weren't even in his company, much less platoon, but they obviously needed help. In spite of all the running he had to do to catch up, his canvas bags flapping at his side, Desmond finished the march with the platoon. Lined up, waiting for dismissal, three men keeled over, out cold. Desmond went to their aid. When he had finished with them, all the other men in the platoon were in their bunks with their shoes off. Desmond did not get a chance even to sit down. He checked every man to see if there was anything he could do to help. That morning some of the men had jeered at him, called him preacher, made derisive remarks. Now, while they lay back exhausted, the slender medic knelt by their bunks and treated their feet.

There was no jeering at Desmond Doss in the barracks that night. He had proved himself. He was one of them now, a fully accepted member of Company B.

As training continued, the three company aid men were drawn closer together. One was Clarence C. Glenn, Jr., a round-faced young man with a big smile which revealed a gold filling in his front tooth. The other aid man was James A. Dorris, also a likable chap but more serious. Both Glenn and Dorris were married, and when Dorothy came to Columbia to be with Desmond, the three couples frequently visited with each other.

Clarence Glenn was the first real live Catholic Desmond had ever known, and Desmond the first Seventh-day Adventist, the first fundamentalist, Glenn had ever been close to. Though some of their comments might have horrified a theologian, still they spent many happy hours discussing their beliefs.

"I just don't see why you make such a fuss about Saturday and Sunday," Glenn said. "Sure, I know what the commandment says, but if practically everybody goes to church on Sunday rather than Saturday, there must be some good reason for it."

"There is a reason, but it's not a good one," Desmond said. "It dates back to the fourth century and a fellow named Constantine. He was a Roman emperor, and a Christian. But most of the Roman subjects those days were pagans, sun worshipers, who observed the sun's day, or Sunday, the first day of the week. Constantine got this great idea that he'd make Sunday a Christian holiday too, and attract all these people. If he couldn't lick 'em, he'd join 'em."

"What happened to Saturday?" Glenn asked.

"Oh, he kept that too," Desmond said.

"You mean he introduced the five-day week," Glenn said with a big grin, his gold tooth flashing.

"Yeah, I guess he did," Desmond agreed, but he didn't smile. He didn't like to make jokes about religion. "Anyhow, they observed both days for, oh, centuries. Originally Saturday was kind of solemn and gradually people began observing Sunday more. Finally the only people who kept the Sabbath were the Jews, just as they'd been doing all along."

"But look, Doss," Glenn objected. In the 77th Division it was always "Doss" and "Glenn"; first names didn't exist. "I just thought of something else. Isn't it hard for you guys to get jobs? I mean, suppose the boss wants you to work Saturday?"

"It's a problem, all right, but we usually find that the Lord works these things out." Desmond paused. How could he tell his friend of his own personal, subjective experience with Sabbath keeping?

From the beginning it was all tied in with the love and inspiration his mother had given him. Being cuddled in her lap, listening to her read and relate stories from the Bible, remained one of his fondest memories.

Desmond's mother had been raised as an Adventist, but his father had not. He smoked and, on occasion, drank. He approved of his wife's religion and found much merit in it, but he put off joining the church himself. One time during the booming twenties Tom Doss asked his employer, a building contractor, whether if he became a Seventh-day Adventist and would no longer work on Saturdays he could keep his job. The boss said No, and that settled the issue for some time.

The depression came, and virtually no new construction was going on in Lynchburg; Tom Doss was lucky if he could find work any day. Mrs. Doss worked in a shoe factory and the children brought home whatever change they could earn from odd jobs until they were old enough to go to work.

Mrs. Doss and the three children continued to go to church on the Sabbath, and Mr. Doss joined them whenever he could. One Saturday they attended a small church near Lynchburg where Elder Lester Coon was pastor. He was a fiery speaker who said what he believed whether the congregation liked it or not.

In his sermon that Sabbath was one sentence that struck home. He seemed to be looking directly at Tom Doss when he said, "To me any man who doesn't stand up for what he thinks is right is a plain old spaghetti back." Desmond saw his father's back stiffen. For years he had supported his wife and children in their choice of religion; he obviously thought it was right. But he had not stood up for it himself.

Tom Doss joined the church. He quit smoking and drinking. And he was almost immediately put to another test. There had been no work for him for weeks. On Wednesday the boss came to him and asked him to do a small renovation job which would take about two days. He put in Thursday and Friday on the job, but still a few hours' work remained to be done. Doss told the boss frankly that he would not complete the work on the Sabbath; it must wait until Monday. He would not even come in Saturday to get his pay. Then he waited. As far as he knew, the boss might refuse to pay him for the work he had already done.

"That's all right, Tom," the boss said. "Finish it up Monday. Your money will be ready when you finish."

From then on Tom Doss was a devout Adventist and a determined Sabbath keeper. And the strange thing was that from that point on he always had plenty of work Monday through Friday. It was the turning point for the Doss family. "So you see," Desmond told Glenn, winding up the story, "God took care of things in His own way, and it all worked out just right."

"Well, you still do a lot of things I don't want to do," Glenn said. "You really make it rough on yourself. You send ten percent of your paycheck to your church. You wouldn't smoke a cigarette or take a drink if your life depended on it. You won't even eat a pork chop!"

"It's all written in the Bible, yours as well as mine," Desmond said. "Pork is unclean, so is shellfish. I don't know what either one tastes like, so it isn't much of a hardship not to eat them."

"Yeah, but the Bible doesn't say one word about cigarettes or bourbon whiskey."

"Maybe not, but in his first letter to the Corinthians Paul said, 'Ye are the temple of God.' That's what we go on, that the body is the temple of God, and we won't defile the temple with nicotine or alcohol or even coffee or tea. I don't think I'm missing much there, either. I used to smoke corn-silk cigarettes when I was a kid, and sometimes a cigarette butt, but all they did was make me cough. One time I took some cough syrup for a cold and the alcohol in it made me so dizzy I couldn't stand up. Once was enough."

Again Desmond paused. How could he explain to this happy-go-lucky buddy of his that, even if the abstinences did seem harsh, the positive attributes of Adventism made such minor sacrifices worthwhile? He was no gloomy gus; Adventists are a happy group of people. They work toward a goal, a positive, attainable goal, with a reward so great that the imagination can hardly picture it.

For the Adventist also takes literally the word of Christ in the twenty-fourth chapter of Matthew, fourteenth verse: "And this gospel of the kingdom shall be preached in all the world for a witness unto all nations; and then shall the end come."

They interpret this to mean that when the word of the coming of Christ has been made known to everyone, then Christ will come again. The world will end, and the faithful, those who have led Christian lives and made it possible for the gospel to be spread, will live in a heavenly happiness that is absolute, forever. The Adventist has the unmatchable goal of complete security, throughout eternity.

"Isn't that worth a cigarette, or a drink of liquor, or a shrimp cocktail?" Desmond asked. And Glenn smiled his golden smile, punched his buddy lightly on the arm, and suggested they start over to the mess hall for chow.

Out of such discussions grew greater understanding. Another result, of great benefit to the men of Company B, was the arrangement by which Glenn worked Saturdays for Doss so that he could go to church and Doss worked Sundays for Glenn so that he could go to mass. Instead of a reluctant medic on duty against his will, the men of the company found an eager, solicitous young man on hand every day in the week. It became a part of the *esprit de corps* of the company. The men stopped going to the battalion infirmary for minor ailments, preferring to stay with their buddies, confident that their three conscientious medics would take good care of them right there in the company area.

Now the entire division was beginning to pull together as a team. It was shaping up into a fine fighting unit with spirit and pride. It was sent on for further training—to the Louisiana maneuvers for simulated combat conditions, to Arizona for desert training, to Pennsylvania and West Virginia for mountain training.

Dorothy followed Desmond wherever she could. In Louisiana the only place she could find to stay was a dreary room in a dilapidated farmhouse. Another soldier's wife shared the same room. When their husbands could join them, the two couples divided the room by hanging a blanket down the middle.

One Sabbath the division was twenty-five miles from Shreveport, the nearest town. Desmond hitchhiked a ride in with a farmer in an old Ford, but after church he could find no way to get back. Military police picked him up and held him overnight along with a group of drunks and troublemakers. A truck from the regiment picked him up in the stockade next day, and he had to explain to his commanding officer that the only thing he had done wrong was go to church.

By now Major Steinman, commanding the medical battalion, had become so infuriated over the Sabbath issue that he refused to give Desmond his pass to go to church, refused him permission to ask for a pass again, and refused to allow him to go to a higher authority on the matter.

"If you give me the slightest provocation, Doss," the major said, "I'll have you court-martialed."

Desmond knew he meant it. The slightest misstep and he was in trouble. He did not go into town to church that week. Dorothy was staying in the farmhouse nearby, and the two of them went out into a cow pasture and held their own services.

Though Desmond had now earned the respect of the men in B Company, he was still having a hard time with the officers of the medical battalion. Even regimental and division officers got into the hassle. During an important field exercise in which several divisions were involved, Desmond, as usual, asked to be relieved of duties on the Sabbath and to be permitted to go to town to church. The next thing he knew he was told to report to a dusty crossroads in the maneuver area. There, in a command car, were two full colonels, one lieutenant colonel, and a major, all waiting for this one soldier who only wanted to go to church.

It was Lieutenant Colonel Thomas B. Manuel, the regimental executive officer, who did most of the talking. Desmond was respectful and very sorry that these high-ranking officers had to take time away from their important duties to discuss religion with a private. But he was adamant. He wouldn't play war on the Sabbath.

"But I thought you could take care of the sick and the injured on the Sabbath," the colonel said.

"Yes, sir, I believe that it is permissible to do good on the Sabbath, and give medical aid to anyone who needs it," Desmond said. "But colonel, we've run this very same exercise four times now, and nobody's been hurt yet."

Finally the brass gave up and permitted him to go into town and take Dorothy to church.

He hitched a ride with an ambulance, which took him to the camp. It was deserted, except for the guards. Desmond's barracks was locked up tight, except for one window right over his bed. Desmond considered this the result of a direct intervention by God, for surely He would not want His devoted subject to go to young people's meeting sweaty and dirty in fatigues. Desmond carried on God's will by getting a fire ladder and crawling in that unlocked window.

And just then the guard came by. Desmond explained the situation to him from the window.

"Do you need that ladder to get out again?" the guard asked.

"Well, no," Desmond said.

"Then I'm going to put it away before somebody sees it and we both get in trouble," the guard said. "Now you hurry up and get cleaned and dressed and out of here."

Desmond appeared at the meeting that night showered, shaved, and dressed in a fresh uniform. Dorothy was there, waiting for him. Together they gave thanks to the Lord for helping Desmond keep the Sabbath and attend church.

The Division moved to the desert country in Arizona and, after several weeks of maneuvers, settled down far out in the desert. The nearest town was Buckeye, where Dorothy lived in the home of an Adventist doctor and his wife. They had an air-conditioned home, the only comfortable place for miles. Desmond was able to get his Sabbath pass again, but how would he get to town?

A railroad went by, but some soldier-passengers had damaged a train and soldiers were no longer permitted to ride. The only other way to leave camp was by truck across the desert, to Phoenix or Yuma, each a hundred or so miles away. Buckeye was only fifty. Desmond obtained permission from regimental headquarters to ride the train if the railroad would let him. The station agent was perfectly willing to sell a round-trip ticket to this clean-looking young man who wanted only to go to church. And so every Friday, while the other members of the division who had received a pass were jouncing across the desert in trucks, Desmond rode into Buckeye by air-conditioned train and participated in quiet private services with Dorothy and a group of other young people.

Desert training shortened tempers from the top to the bottom. It was a cruel experience that had deleterious effects on the entire division. At that time the United States Army, influenced by operations in the North African desert, was placing extreme emphasis on reducing the amount of water used by the troops. Water, this most common liquid, becomes a precious commodity when it is in short supply. Each unit was severely limited in the amount of water it could have each day. The water was delivered to the company area in fifty-gallon drums in open trucks. Some of the precious stuff would slosh over on the sandy floor of the truck and run out under the tail gate. Men would run after the truck, catch the water in their helmets, and drink it, mud, sand, and all.

On long hikes over the vicious desert, men would fall out through sheer dehydration. Medics were not given extra water, and sometimes Desmond and the others had to share some of their own. Desmond was already severely penalized, for, although his individual consumption was computed in the coffee and tea served at meals, he did not drink these either.

Under such conditions it was easy to get excited about water. One day the men in the company came running to Desmond with the report that Lieutenant Gornto, who was temporarily in command, was making no provision to apportion out the water in the platoon's existing supply. This was a most important procedure. Each morning at a certain time the water trucks would come around to replenish the supply. Kitchen barrels and individual canteens should be filled from what was left in the company water containers before they were refilled. Otherwise they would lose that much water.

"But the lieutenant's just sittin' there doin' nothin'!" the men told Doss excitedly. "We got to get that water!"

Though Doss was only a private, as a medical soldier he had prescribed responsibilities in matters of sanitation and health. He looked into the situation and found out that the men were right. He then felt morally obligated to screw up his courage, approach the lieutenant, and tell him what to do.

Gornto received him casually. He looked tired. "Don't worry about it, Doss," he said. "I'll take care of it."

Doss saluted and left, but still nothing was done. It was now almost time for the trucks to arrive. Doss ran to the headquarters of the medical battalion to report the matter to a medical officer. The officer on duty happened to be a close buddy of Lieutenant Gornto's. Doss felt that the whole thing was an exercise in futility, but again he felt obligated to carry the matter as far as he could.

The medical officer listened to Doss's report. He was obligated to take some action in the matter, and he grudgingly assured Doss that he would do so. By the time Doss returned to the company area, Gornto had had the water distributed. It was a moral victory for Desmond, and the men respected him for it. Gornto never referred to it again, but Desmond was naturally somewhat uneasy with him from then on. It does not make for smooth relations with your platoon leader to blow the whistle on him.

To make the episode still worse, what Doss had not known was that Gornto and his jeep driver, Edward J. Panek, had spent most of the night looking for the water truck. Gornto had known all along that it would be later than usual.

The men of the 77th existed in an atmosphere of parched heat, irritability, misunderstanding, and distrust. Conditions were so miserable that desertion was common. Some men fled into the desert and were never seen again. Even one of the chaplains went AWOL! Only in such an environment could the next episode in Private Doss's war with the Army have taken place. Going into the hot headquarters tent of the medical battalion to pick up his pass one Friday, he noticed that the chair-borne commandos, the pencil pushers, were giving each other knowing looks. The top sergeant, who reflected with magnification the commanding officer's disapproval of Doss, handed over the pass with an unpleasant grin.

"I won't be doing this much longer, Doss," he said. "Arrangements are being made so that you can have all your Saturdays off from now on."

Something was in the wind, Desmond knew. He went to one of the officers of the battalion to find out what was going on.

"I've got good news for you, Private Doss," he said. "You're getting out of the Army. We've discussed your case at length and have come to the conclusion that you are eligible for discharge under the terms of Section Eight. You'll appear before the discharge committee this morning. Go to your tent. You'll be summoned when they're ready for you."

Desmond's spirits went up—then down. He was human, and he had had enough of this desert. His nose was swollen and inflamed from the constant dust; his eyes were watering. The officers were down on him; he could never relax. He'd had enough. He was ready to go home.

But "Section Eight," he knew, referred to mental instability. And Desmond Doss did not believe that, just because he wanted to go to church on Saturday, he was a nut.

The discharge committee, composed of five medical officers, sat around a folding table out in the open. The papers were already made out. The chairman told Desmond what he already knew, that he was up for discharge.

"Why Section Eight?" he stammered. He was one lone private facing five military doctors who thought he was crazy. What could he say? "Hasn't my work been satisfactory?"

"Well, yes, it has," the chairman admitted. "But everyone else in this unit is training seven days a week. Your refusal to train with the rest of the men on Saturdays means that you are missing valuable training. You can miss something important which could keep you from doing your job properly. A man's life could be at stake. Even your own life could be in danger."

Desmond pointed out how he and Clarence Glenn had worked out an efficient system by which one of them was on duty during the weekend, and that Company B had the lowest number of men on sick call in the regiment. Committee members might as well not have heard him. Obviously they wanted him to agree to accept the discharge without protest. But this he could not do.

"You say my work is satisfactory," he said, "so the only grounds you have for my discharge is my keeping the Sabbath. I'd be a very poor Christian to accept a discharge implying that I was mentally off purely because of my religion. When I'm called upon to treat my fellow soldiers on the Sabbath, I will do it, and willingly. I don't believe that I am missing anything of importance by not being here on Saturdays, but if I do miss anything, even something that might endanger my life, well, I'll just take that chance."

Desmond paused for breath. "Sir," he said softly, "please believe me. I know that if I keep God's commandments, He will give me wisdom and understanding equal to those who receive training on His holy day."

That answer stopped the Section Eight discharge, right there. It was obvious that Washington would never approve a discharge given on purely religious grounds. Desmond remained in the Army, on the desert—a strange victory. His situation was even worse than before, for it was all over the division that the officers of the medical battalion had tried to railroad a good soldier out of the Army, and had gotten themselves chewed out instead. This did not increase Desmond's popularity with the brass.

Finally, now, this desert training hell was coming to a close. Word came down that the division's next stop would be the Indiantown Gap Military Reservation in Pennsylvania. Trees, grass, plenty of water, and no more sand. Elation swept through the entire division.

At noon Desmond Doss came in from the field, hot and dry but happy in the knowledge that soon this would end. Waiting for him was an order to report to regimental headquarters. And there he was told that he had been officially transferred out of the medics, into the headquarters company of the regiment. He was in the infantry again. His enemies in the medical battalion had gotten rid of him in another way.

In a kind of daze, Desmond went to his tent to get his medical equipment and turn it in. Then he would report to his new company. He couldn't find a strap. Suddenly he realized that that one piece of canvas was all that stood between him and the infantry, that now his troubles were really beginning. He fell on his knees.

"Help me, O Lord," he begged. "Give me wisdom so that I will know what to do."

He remembered Captain Stanley, who had helped him before. The missing strap gave him time to visit the chaplain, but Captain Stanley could give him only sympathy and good wishes. Finally Desmond found the strap and, knowing he was in for trouble, turned in his equipment. One of his friends, T/4 March Howell, told him good-bye.

"And say, Doss," Howell added, "I just made a ten-dollar bet with your new company commander. He said he'd have you carrying a gun in thirty days. I bet you wouldn't."

"You know I don't approve of gambling, sergeant," Desmond said. "I don't want either one of you to lose. But I'm not going to carry a gun."

Desmond reported to his new company commander, Lieutenant Walter G. Cosner.[3] The lieutenant had been primed that a troublemaker was being transferred to his platoon, and he was ready for him. Doss was already assigned to the pioneer ammunition section, and the carbine he was to carry was waiting for him.

"Private Doss," the lieutenant said, "take this carbine."

Desmond instantly realized the cat-and-mouse game the lieutenant was playing with him. Though as a conscientious objector he was officially exempt from bearing arms, no soldier is exempt from the obligation to obey the direct command of a commissioned officer. The lieutenant was out to make him either take the weapon or be court-martialed.

"I'm sorry, sir," Doss said, "but according to my religious convictions, I cannot bear arms."

Again the lieutenant ordered Doss to take the rifle, and again Doss declined, phrasing his answer in such a way that it was not a direct refusal.

The lieutenant tired of playing games with the rifle, and picked up a .45 automatic pistol. "You can take this, Doss," he said. "This isn't really a weapon."

"Then what is it, sir?" Doss asked. The lieutenant played the game with a trench knife, then an ammunition kit. Doss declined both, again without making a direct refusal.

---

3   A pseudonym.

"Look, Doss," the lieutenant said, "I don't want you to kill anybody. I just want you to train with these weapons, like everybody else."

"I would rather put my faith in the Lord than confidence in a carbine," Desmond said.

The lieutenant leaned forward. "You're married. Now suppose somebody was raping your wife. Wouldn't you use a gun?"

"I wouldn't have one."

"What would you do, then?"

"I wouldn't just stand there," Doss said sharply. "I wouldn't use a gun, and I wouldn't kill, but he'd sure wish he was dead when I got through with him."

The conflict was interrupted by the move to Indiantown Gap. There the lieutenant had the last word. Doss was placed on permanent KP and given the job of scrubbing the pots and pans. The unrelieved exposure to the harsh lye in the soap left his hands raw and bleeding. He was refused a pass to leave the company area, which meant that it would be useless for Dorothy to come to Indiantown Gap.

A telegram arrived from home. His younger brother Harold was home on his last furlough before going overseas with the Navy. This would be the last chance for the whole family to be together. About this time several men in the platoon, including Doss, became eligible for a furlough and they all put in for it. The lieutenant had the papers prepared and lined up the men, presenting each one with his papers. When he came to Doss he placed the papers in his outstretched hand.

"You haven't qualified with your weapon yet, have you, Doss?" he asked. "Well, there's a regulation that no man gets his furlough until he does."

He snatched the papers back and tore them up.

Desmond went to the chaplain and all the way to the colonel of the regiment, but both told him there was nothing they could do. Sadly he walked over to the telephone in the Post Exchange and called his family long distance.

"I can't come home," he said. Then he choked up. He was in serious trouble. He might never see his brother again. He might never see any of his loved ones again. The way things were going, he could wind up in prison. He stood there clutching the phone, unable to speak, as the seconds he was paying for ticked by.

"Desmond," his mother was crying. "Desmond! What's the matter? Where are you? Desmond!"

Finally he controlled himself and poured out the whole story.

Next morning Desmond was up to his elbows in lye soap when he got word to report to the medical battalion. Major Steinman was waiting for him. "Welcome back," he said.

The top sergeant said, "Go report to your old company. You're back in the medics."

"Can I have a furlough?" Desmond asked, and explained his home situation. In any event, he was due a furlough.

But things had not changed. Desmond would have to wait for a furlough. He could have a three-day pass—in which case, no furlough.

"I'll take the pass," Desmond sighed.

He started for home immediately. When he arrived he found out what had happened. His father had gotten in touch with Carlyle B. Haynes, chairman of the church's War Service Commission in Washington. Haynes called the regimental commander, Colonel Stephen S. Hamilton. "I understand you're having some difficulty up there, colonel," he had said pleasantly. "Is it necessary for me to come there and look into it?"

"Oh, no, not at all," the colonel said. "Whatever it is, we can straighten it out right here."

Desmond had been transferred back to the medics immediately after. However, just in case, Haynes sent to both the regimental commander and to Doss copies of documents signed by both President Roosevelt, commander in chief, and General George C. Marshall, chief of staff, affirming that conscientious objectors would not have to bear arms.

With Desmond now definitely in the medical battalion, 307th Regiment, assigned to Company B, the division continued training, at Indiantown Gap, a West Virginia training area, and at Camp Pickett, Virginia. Doss's unit drove up into the West Virginia mountains in open trucks wearing khakis, and into seven inches of snow.

While they trained in the mountains there, a minor episode occurred which was to assume great importance later, in combat. Several training periods were given over to learning how to tie knots which would be useful in mountain climbing. Through his membership in the Junior Missionary Volunteers, Desmond was thoroughly familiar with the knots, but he pitched in and practiced just the same. One day there was a shortage of rope and Doss did not have one to practice on. Two men were sharing one long rope, one at each end, and Desmond took the middle part, doubled it, and practiced with that. When he tied a bowline, a loop that will not slip, in the doubled line, he found that he had two loops rather than one. Both held securely. He had never seen this done before and he tucked it away in his mind.

In the second week of March 1944, the 77th Division made its last move in the United States. Well trained, at full strength, with good morale and determined to prove themselves in battle, the men of the Statue of Liberty Division boarded special troop trains at Camp Pickett and headed west toward the Pacific and the Japanese. Dorothy, along with many other wives, was permitted to come to the company area to say good-bye. She and Desmond had said their good-byes in the privacy of the camp guest-house the night before. Now they could only look into each other's eyes and repeat again, "I love you, I love you."

The next major city to the west was Lynchburg. Desmond was on KP, peeling potatoes in a baggage car, when he began to recognize landmarks on the outskirts of his hometown. He knew that the train would pass close to the Doss home. He also knew that his father liked to watch the trains go by. Desmond called the other men on KP with him, and they all got mops and brooms and stationed themselves in the open double doors. Sure enough, there was the familiar house and the familiar figure on the front porch.

"OK, now!" Desmond hollered, and his buddies began waving their mops and brooms. Mr. Doss waved back, with no idea that he was waving to his own son.

On the spur of the moment Desmond took a paper napkin and hastily wrote on it, "Dear Mom and Dad, I'm on the way. Pray for me."

He tied a handkerchief around the paper, wrote his parent's name and address on the outside, and threw it off the train in hopes it would be found and taken to his parents. (It was, the next day.)

The train rattled on through Lynchburg, over a high trestle, toward the Pacific. Desmond looked longingly back toward the scenes of his childhood. Two good-byes in one day would take a lot out of any soldier. His spirits, already low, suddenly hit bottom. He had the sudden fear that he would never see his loved ones again. The train was still crossing over the trestle. *I might as well jump off*, he thought disconsolately.

Instead, Desmond reached in his pocket and pulled out his most precious possession. It was the Bible Dorothy had given him after they were married. In it she had marked a truly appropriate verse, 1 Corinthians 10:13, for encouragement. He read it again: "There hath no temptation taken you but such as is common to man: but God is faithful, who will not suffer you to be tempted above that ye are able; but will with the temptation also make a way to escape, that ye may be able to bear it."

Then he turned to the first page. There was a letter she had written in the Bible before presenting it to him. As the train carried him westward, each click of the wheels beneath him taking him farther and farther away from the woman he loved, Desmond read, as he had so many times before, the words she had written.

November 22, 1942

Dearest Desmond,

As you read and study the precious promises found in the word of God contained in this little Bible, may you be strengthened in whatever trials may come to you.

May your faith in God bring comfort and peace of heart to you, that you may never be sad or lonely no matter how dark the way seems.

If we do not meet another time on this earth, we have the assurance of a happy meeting place in heaven. May God in His mercy grant us both a place there.

Your loving wife,

Dorothy

Desmond Doss closed the Bible and put it back in his pocket over his heart. What a wonderful letter. Once again he drew courage and comfort from it. He sighed and, as the train picked up speed, he went back to his potatoes. And so he was off to war.

CHAPTER 3

COMBAT!

A heavy sea was running and the big transport ship pitched and rolled like a crazy sea monster. At her side, but far beneath, the landing craft bobbed and wallowed erratically in the gray-green Pacific. A driving rain beat against the ponchos, helmets, and unprotected faces of the men. It obscured the distant shoreline, and the howling wind muffled the sounds of artillery fire and exploding shells.

"OK, Second Platoon, start loading!" Lieutenant Willis A. J. Munger, the fresh-faced young officer who was replacing Lieutenant Gornto temporarily, slung his leg over the rail. The other men followed. Now it was Doss's turn. On his back was his field pack, his canteen and shovel on his belt. From each shoulder hung a big canvas first-aid kit. Carrying more than seventy-five pounds, the driving rain beating into his face, his cold, wet hands clutching the rail, the ship bucking and rearing, he felt with his feet for the thick rope of the landing net slung on the side of the ship. He found a foothold and began the long climb down to the landing craft.

"All aboard, sir!" a voice shouted.

"Cast off!"

The boat slowly moved away from the parent ship and headed toward the rendezvous point, pitching and tossing in the waves. Now up, with a swoosh, now down with a sickening lift in the pit of the stomach.

It wasn't long before nausea gripped even the toughest men. Lieutenant Munger, younger than most of the men he commanded, tried to keep his dignity, but his face was turning green.

Wretched and miserable in the open boat in the driving rain, Desmond Doss and his 2d Platoon proceeded to their first action. It was a dramatic, daring operation. If successful, it would extend the American spearhead a full thousand miles deep into the Japanese-held island area between Japan itself and the Caroline Islands. The 77th's objective was Guam, largest of the Marianas and an American possession which the Japanese had taken shortly after Pearl Harbor.

Ever since the arrival in Hawaii on April 1, 1944, two years to the day after Desmond's induction, the 77th had been training for this operation, the assault on a fortified island. Part of the preparation had involved the arming of all medical soldiers. Tragic experience had shown the American army that the Japanese were instructed to seek out and kill medical soldiers in the correct assumption that it would affect morale. The battalion executive officer, Colonel Gerald G. Cooney, had ordered Doss to carry a weapon, and on his refusal, had recommended that he be returned to the States. Captain Vernon, B Company's CO, had interceded at the last moment, and Desmond remained with the company.

Now, approaching Guam, Desmond was not so sure that staying had been a good idea. It was an actual relief when the LCI scraped the coral reef some 400 yards from the beach. The ramp was lowered, and one of the men gingerly dropped himself into the water. It was up to his chin. Doss went in up to his armpits. Some of the shorter men, weighed down with pack, rifle, and ammunition, had to be helped on the long, sloshing walk to shore.

Weakened by nausea, exhausted after wading a quarter of a mile, the men of B Company assembled on the beach. The American soldiers who had fallen on the first assault had been removed, but Japanese bodies lay everywhere. They lay in twisted positions, on front and back, in and out of mudholes. Desmond tried not to look at the bodies. The Army had tried to teach him to hate the enemy, but it had not been successful.

Desmond checked with his buddies, Glenn and Dorris. They had reached shore safely. With Captain Vernon at the head, the company started a five-mile hike to their bivouac area. Under the combination of heavy tanks and the tropical downpour, the trail was a series of mudholes, some waist deep. When they reached the area, the men were at the limit of their endurance. Desmond opened his package of K rations. It contained a chunk of cheese with bacon in it. As he could not eat pork, he gave it away to those who could and started munching on the hard, tasteless crackers that came in the package. The GIs called them dog biscuits. The K-ration package also contained cigarettes and coffee. Not approving of either, Desmond threw them both away—a moral luxury that would not last too many days. They could be traded for another dog biscuit or a candy bar.

COMBAT!

The first battalion of the 307th Infantry, which included Company B, was being held in reserve, and for four days the cold, wet soldiers sat huddled in their ponchos by day, shivered in holes that had to be constantly bailed out by night. Their uniforms, green cotton fatigues, never dried out. Their feet were always wet.

Then came orders to move out, and to move out fast. The mission was to cross the narrow island to the east, then drive northward to the crossroads of Barrigada. This was a vital point. A functioning well was located there. In spite of all that rain, the invasion forces were running out of water. There were few wells on this coral island. Barrigada had to be taken.

It was about eight miles across the island, another five up to Barrigada. These are crow's-flight distances; the actual mileage, around hills and over winding jungle trails, was much further. Nor was the terrain secure. In the haste to get water, the forward elements were driving straight through, bypassing Japanese snipers, rearguard patrols, and even large pockets of the enemy. The battalion traveled as a self-contained unit. As it passed through, the jungle closed up after it. There was nobody behind.

Desmond chose his position at about two thirds back from the head of the platoon. It would be pointless for him to march at the front, not only because he was a high-priority target, but because he could not watch his men from there. But it would also be unwise to bring up the rear.

They pushed along briskly. An occasional sniper's bullet whistled by, but no one in the platoon was injured. The men watched where they put their feet, and were careful to touch nothing. They had been warned against booby traps. The Japanese even booby-trapped their own dead. Roll a corpse over, and a grenade would go off.

But of course no Japanese would drop an American fountain pen. One of the men saw it, lying bright and shiny by the trail. He was a happy-go-lucky, impulsive kid.

"Hey, look at that," he cried, "a fountain pen!"

Three of the men who were near him stopped and joined him as he picked it up. Suddenly an explosion shook the jungle. The pen had triggered a white phosphorus grenade.

Desmond heard the cry—"Medic! Doss! Doss!" He hurried forward. He smelled the burning flesh before he reached the men; white phosphorus sticks to the skin as it burns with a white heat. The man who had picked up the pen had taken most of the blast. His torso was a bloody mess. The other men were suffering from severe burns and wounds caused by pieces of flying metal.

Desmond slung off his first-aid kits and went to work. The man who had activated the booby trap was in the worst shape. He had lost a lot of blood, was critically burned, and was already in a state of shock. Desmond stanched the flow of blood and treated the burns. Another man was also in bad shape. Desmond treated him next. The other two were better off. By the time he had finished, four litter bearers had come up. They would carry the two seriously injured men back to the battalion aid station; the other two were classified as walking wounded and traveled under their own power.

Not until it was over did Desmond realize that he had treated his first casualties. He had not panicked. If the two badly injured men lived, it would be because of his prompt, efficient action. Before starting after his unit, Desmond paused to give thanks to the Lord for enabling him to do his job.

Desmond caught up with the 2d Platoon before nightfall. They were getting close to the main Japanese forces now, passing abandoned equipment and bivouac areas where the fires were still warm. That night seven Japanese were killed trying to infiltrate the company area.

There had been no official water for days, and the men had gotten what they could where they could. As a result nearly everyone suffered from nausea, headaches, and diarrhea. They could appreciate the need to capture Barrigada.

The battle order came down. The 2d Platoon was in the very center of the battalion front, headed on a crossroads. They dashed through the jungle. Suddenly Pfc Julian R. Perez, the platoon scout, started firing. A light machine gun opened up. Pfc Angelo B. Pacella went down. Lieutenant Munger halted the advance and sent a group of men around on each side to envelope the machine gun. They knocked it out, and the advance continued.

The battle grew hotter. Several companies were now involved, all of them blasting away. The Japanese returned the fire. Doss scooped out a little hole and made himself as small as possible. Down the road he saw a green-clad American soldier jump up and start running forward in a crouching position. Suddenly he went down and lay motionless. Out of nowhere an officer, obviously the fallen soldier's company commander, came running, standing straight up, waving his hands and shouting the man's name.

Desmond began running toward him too, but he kept low. The soldier was lying on his face where he had fallen. Desmond crossed one of the soldier's legs over the other and turned him so that he lay face up. Blood was all over the man's chest. His captain looked on helplessly. Desmond took both hands and ripped the fatigue jacket open. A shell fragment had torn a big hole in the victim's chest.

The medic knew there was little he could do, but he opened up his kit and took out a large battle dressing just the same. As he was putting it in place, the soldier let out his last dying breath. He was dead.

Desmond breathed one short, quick, but fervent prayer, then he and the captain sped back toward cover. Not until after Desmond had dived into the jungle underbrush and gasped for breath did he realize that he had just lost his first American soldier.

In front of Barrigada lay a large clearing. On the other side stood a deserted green shack. "That looks like good protection," Munger said. "Let's take it."

Munger and Perez, crouching low and zigzagging, ran across the field to the shack. The other men of the platoon, in groups of twos and threes, followed. Suddenly an enemy tank, the machine gun on its turret hammering out fire and death, came through the village and roared up to the regimental command post, leaving wounded and dead men in its wake. Two men from the 2d Platoon had been hit. The Japanese started pasting the green shack with mortar and artillery.

"Anyone who wants to go can leave—I wouldn't blame you," Munger told his men. "But I'm sticking."

The men stuck with him. Sergeant Charles J. Kunze volunteered to go for reinforcements. He dashed across the open field and reported the situation to Captain Vernon.

"Tell Munger to come back," Vernon said. "That shack isn't worth it."

Kunze dashed across the field again, delivered the message. As other members of the company, under fire, covered them, Munger led his men out of the shack. He was hit and fell—dead. Perez and Kunze were wounded. But the Japanese attack was beaten off. The next morning the village was taken, along with the well and a small reservoir of water.

After the Americans secured the village, they collected the dead and placed them together. Some of the native Chamorros had also lost their lives in the battle. Desmond was walking near the collection area when he heard a slight moan. He thought he saw one of the natives stir. These people had been of great help to the Americans. Desmond went to the man and knelt by his side. He could feel no pulse. He placed his finger gently on the carotid artery in the neck. There was the slightest sensation of movement. The man was still alive!

Desmond examined him, found the wound, and treated it. He then checked all the bodies. Another, an American, was also alive. Desmond had both men taken to the battalion aid station. From then on he never gave up on any man until positive he was dead.

"Haven't you got enough to do, taking care of our own men?" Glenn asked. "Why try to resurrect these natives?"

"Because it's not up to me to judge whether one of God's children should live or die," Desmond said. "That is a decision for the Lord to make, not me. I believe that I should do everything in my power to help all men hold on to life."

"Suppose they aren't fit to live?"

"Well, the way I look at it," Desmond said, "is that anybody who isn't fit to live surely isn't fit to die! What worse fate could possibly happen to any mortal than to die when he doesn't deserve to live? That would seal his doom forever. No matter how evil a person may be he deserves to live, for he may discover the teachings of Jesus and be saved!"

At Barrigada the 307th lost eighty-five men killed and wounded. The miserable conditions—constant rain, polluted water, clouds of flies and mosquitoes—also took their toll in sickness.

But the push against the Japanese continued. Patrols constantly probed ahead of the advancing line. If they found no resistance, the larger bodies of troops moved up. If they met resistance, then the decision had to be made by higher echelons when to attack and in what strength.

Whenever the 2d Platoon was assigned a patrol mission, Desmond went along with his men. His old friend Sergeant Howell, one of the senior noncoms at the battalion aid station, heard that Desmond was going out on patrol with the dogfaces.

"Have you lost your mind, Doss?" he demanded. "It's not your job to get killed. Your job is to stay alive so that you can help these men when they get hit. If Captain Vernon or anybody else tries to send you on patrol you tell him it's not your duty."

"It may not be my duty," Desmond told him, "but it's what I believe in. I know these men; they're my buddies. They have families, some have wives and children. If they're hurt I want to be there to take care of them."

He continued to go out on patrol, slipping noiselessly through the jungles, maintaining constant visual contact with the men in front of him, peering about for any suspicious activity, ever alert to the danger of booby traps and mines. If the patrol was fired upon and a man was hit, the other men would close in and cover Doss while he administered first aid. Then they'd all retreat together, helping the wounded man to safety.

Even when they encountered no opposition, the patrols were more efficient with Doss along. He gave the men confidence. Even the bravest soldier has a horror of being wounded and left behind, helpless, at the mercy of the enemy. For the enemy had no mercy. But with Doss along that fear was alleviated, for they knew their medic wouldn't leave them.

Captain Vernon and the other officers came to expect Doss to go out with the men. Vernon himself, as brave and as fair as any officer in the Army, went out himself, and he expected no less of any of his men.

And yet friction developed between the brave captain and the brave medic. When a man received a slight wound that might become infected, when he was so sick with fever or diarrhea that he couldn't do his job, Doss insisted that he return to the battalion aid station to be checked by a medical officer. Sometimes the man did not return. Captain Vernon felt that Doss was oversolicitous. He himself would fight on as long as he was conscious, and he expected his men to do the same.

"That man wasn't badly hurt," he raged at Doss one day. "You didn't have to send him back."

"He needed more attention than I could give him, captain," Doss said quietly. "I didn't have any choice."

"You pill rollers are mollycoddling these men," Vernon said. "We're fighting a war up here, not running a hospital."

"Captain," Doss said, "some of these men are so sick they couldn't do you or themselves any good. On patrol they don't know what they're doing. They'll get themselves and the rest of us killed."

In the meantime, pressure was coming on him from another direction. "What's this I hear about you going out on patrols?" Captain Leo Tann, the medical officer at the battalion aid station, said. "You can't do anybody any good if you get shot yourself. Leave the patrols to the riflemen. You stay in the company area where you belong."

Desmond had been at the aid station picking up supplies. When he returned to the company, he found that his platoon had been moved out. He set out through the jungle, trying to overtake them, but he had gone only a couple of hundred yards when another officer in the company saw him.

"Get back, Doss," he said. "There are Japanese all through here."

"But I'm trying to find my platoon," Doss said.

"They're way up ahead now," the officer said. "You'd never make it alive. Get back! That's an order."

Back at the company area, Desmond had a feeling of unease, as though something was going to happen. That night he uttered a special prayer to the Lord for his men. He had never failed to say his daily prayers, incidentally, morning and evening. He even returned thanks when he munched dog biscuits and washed them down with foul-tasting water. But he no longer knelt at all times. On the front there was constant danger of Japanese infiltrating past the company perimeter. Standing orders were to shoot at anything that moved. If Desmond had stuck his head out of his hole he would likely have gotten it shot off. And so, he reasoned, God would hear his prayers whether he was standing, kneeling, or lying shivering in a muddy hole.

That night he asked the Lord that, if it were His will, He give special protection to the men of the 2d Platoon. In the morning Lieutenant George M. Black, who had replaced Lieutenant Munger, burst into the company area with two of his men. All three had been slightly wounded.

"An artillery and mortar barrage zeroed in on us and kept it up all night," Black reported. "Several of our men were hit. They need attention."

Desmond threw his first-aid kits over his shoulders. "I'm ready, sir," he said.

The lieutenant led the medic and a squad of riflemen back to the platoon. Snipers fired on them all the way. Several men were injured and Desmond dressed their wounds. From their description of the barrage, he knew that it was a miracle that any man had lived. Yet of the entire platoon, only one man lost his life. When he had treated the last wounded man, Desmond Doss bowed his head and humbly gave thanks to the Lord for hearing his prayer.

On the way back he was twice as vulnerable to the snipers' bullets, for now he was helping one of his men who hobbled with a leg wound. The two made their way through the jungle with the wounded man hopping on one leg, his arm around Desmond's neck for support. A dozen times bullets whistled through the foliage, and the two dropped to the ground. It was a long trip and a painful one, but they reached the company area safely.

Two days later the company was together again. Again a 2d Platoon patrol went out, this time without their medic. When Captain Vernon learned that Desmond had not accompanied the patrol, he told him to catch up with it. By that time the patrol was deep in the woods. Japanese snipers were all through that area. Even more dangerous, Doss knew, were the green replacements in the patrol. They'd shoot at anything.

"It's too late to go now, captain," Desmond said. "If the Japanese don't get me the new men will."

"Do you refuse to go?" Vernon demanded.

"Captain, I'd just get myself killed, and I'm under orders not to take that kind of chance."

Vernon blew up. "I'm going to have you court-martialed!" he shouted. "You chancre mechanics have to take orders like everybody else."

Desmond hurried to the battalion aid station to report the situation to Captain Tann. The medical officer in turn immediately made a report to regimental headquarters. Tann had heard of Vernon's references to his medics as pill rollers and chancre mechanics and was annoyed with him. There was no court-martial, and Captain Vernon was officially informed that Doss took orders from the medical battalion, not the officers of B Company. The episode officially closed, but Desmond knew it had rankled the captain.

Desmond himself, about this time, learned something about the responsibility of command. The battalion was cleaning up sporadic resistance north of Barrigada. It moved swiftly, as a self-contained unit. The jungle closed up behind it as it passed.

Suddenly shots rang out. Ambush! Four men were seriously wounded. Desmond got to them first and gave them emergency treatment.

By now nearly all the battalion had gone by. What would Desmond do with the wounded men? They could not walk, and he couldn't leave them there. While he worked on them some men came by with litters and dropped four. Then came the rear guard. After that there was nobody except perhaps the Japanese. The rear guard was under the command of an infantry sergeant. Desmond didn't know him, but he knew the sergeant would have to be tough and competent to be entrusted with so critical an assignment.

"I need some of your men to carry these wounded," Doss told him.

"Are you crazy? This is the rear guard. I can't spare any men."

"You've got to. Do you think I'm going to leave these men here to die?"

"I can't help that," the sergeant snapped. "All I know is I can't leave any men."

He was shouting, and Desmond shouted right back. "I'm a medical soldier, and this is an emergency and I'm ordering you to help me carry these wounded American soldiers. And if you don't I'm going to get your name and serial number and you'll be busted right down to a private."

"Well, I've got to ask the lieutenant. He's gone on."

"OK, then, go ask," Desmond agreed, "but leave some men here until you come back."

The sergeant started running up the trail after the lieutenant. The jungle became quiet. There was only a handful of men and the wounded, and they all kept looking about apprehensively. But the sergeant came running back.

"All right," the sergeant panted, "the lieutenant says take what you need, but make it snappy. Let's get out of here."

Four men quickly grabbed the handles of each litter and set off at a quick step along the trail. Desmond stuck with them until he could transfer the casualties, all still alive, to the rear.

The campaign on Guam was drawing to a close. Only mopping-up operations remained. The 77th Division moved into a bivouac area for a rest and to break in the new replacements. And Captain Tann summoned Desmond to the aid station.

"I'm having you transferred out of Company B," he said. "You'll be a litter bearer working out of this aid station. If Captain Vernon doesn't know what to do with the best company aid man in the Army, well, I do."

Desmond packed up his things and moved in with the medical battalion. He had several friends there. One of them was a litter bearer named Herbert Schechter. Herb was a short, chunky fellow with black curly hair. He was quiet, sincere, and religious. Like Desmond, he observed the Sabbath, but as a Jew, not an Adventist. The two young men liked to discuss religion, finding pleasure in their close agreement on many philosophical points.

"Boy, am I glad to see you!" Herb cried. "I'll bet you're not sorry to be out of that outfit."

"No, I guess not," Desmond said. But deep inside he wasn't so sure. Up there with the fighting men he felt he could best serve his fellowmen and his country, and therefore his God. Perhaps it was where he belonged.

Shortly afterward the man who had replaced Doss as company aid man died suddenly with pneumonia. Doss went to Captain Tann and asked to be sent back to Company B.

"Doss, are you crazy?" the captain asked.

"No, sir. I'd just like to go back to my old buddies."

Captain Tann sighed and arranged for the transfer.

CHAPTER 4

ONE BUSY SABBATH

H ey, Doss," one of the new replacements called, "have you heard the latest? Because we've been through two rough campaigns they're gonna make us a reserve of reserves in this next one. That's pretty good, huh?"

Desmond sighed. So many replacements—it was practically a new outfit. He didn't even know this young soldier's name. "Yeah, sounds pretty good," he replied. No point in telling him what the old-timers knew. "Reserve of reserves" sounded good all right, but what it really meant was that the 77th would be held out until the situation was desperate, then thrown into the toughest, bloodiest fighting of all. That's the way it always worked. They had barely finished up the Leyte campaign and here they were getting ready to fight again.

Desmond couldn't help feeling some bitterness. Months before they'd been promised a rest on New Caledonia; well, they hadn't even *seen* New Caledonia. He was now supposed to have a Bronze Star, but he hadn't seen that either. Even if he had it, he could just see himself pinning it on his dirty fatigues.

Captain Tann had taken it on himself to get his men promotions, and now Desmond was a private first class. After almost three years in the Army, he was one grade above the bottom, with a base pay increase from $50 a month to $54. Big deal.

In the spring of 1945, it was obvious to any American in the South Pacific that from here on any operation would be a major, hard-fought struggle. As the Americans came closer to the Japanese homeland, the Japanese resisted fanatically. Wherever the next battle would be, Desmond knew, it would be the fiercest challenge to the division and to himself.

With the rest of the 1st Battalion, Company B left the bivouac area on Leyte and boarded the U.S.S. *Mauntrail*. This was the company's fourth transport. Looking around him, Desmond saw some of the old familiar faces on board—Captain Vernon and Lieutenant Gornto, of course, and Lieutenant Phillips and Lieutenant Onless C. Brister, who'd also seen a lot of action. There were two other Virginians in the company, William S. Carnes and Lewis R. Brooks, whom he knew well, and, of course, his fellow medic Jim Dorris. Some of the noncoms, like Sergeant Kunze, had been given battlefield commissions and transferred as officers to other companies. Privates and Pfc's had been promoted. Joseph R. Potts, Charles C. Edgette, and Clarence O'Connell were sergeants now, on their way up. Staff Sergeant John Maholic, always one of the best-liked men in the company, had proved himself again and again in combat, and was one of the most respected men in the outfit and the most popular.

But the missing faces outnumbered those present. Glenn and Schechter and the others—Desmond quickly pulled his mind away. Such thoughts were dangerous. Northward steamed the convoy, northward until it seemed that Japan itself was just over the horizon. Late in the day of March 23, a big island appeared. It was Okinawa, in the Ryukyus, little more than 500 miles from the southernmost island of Japan. It was common knowledge that the island bristled with weapons and was defended by large numbers of the enemy's finest troops.

Other units of the 77th participated in comparatively minor engagements on the smaller islands surrounding Okinawa. Company B didn't leave the ship, but it was in a constant war of its own. For it was during this period that the Japanese introduced the Kamikazes, or suicide planes. The *Mauntrail* was under constant attack. During one five-minute period the ship shot down three Japanese planes. The *Mauntrail* stayed off the coast of Okinawa for almost a month with its reserve of reserves, fighting off swarms of Kamikazes. Almost with relief the men of the 1st Battalion, 307th Regiment, learned that they would be getting off this ship and going into combat.

"It must be pretty rough or they wouldn't be calling us this soon," one of the men observed.

"It's always rough," Desmond answered. "But with God's help we'll do all right."

Ashore, the men quickly heard many of the gory details of that strange and tragic campaign. The Japanese had convinced the natives that the Americans would torture and slaughter them. Horrified young Americans saw native mothers cut their children's throats, then their own, as the soldiers approached. In a hysterical madness that caught all the civilians on the island, they slaughtered themselves and each other.

The Okinawans buried their dead in large caves marked by strange, ornate entrances. Moving into the front lines, Company B stopped for the night just short of the combat zone. It was a desolate, fought-over area with shot-up tanks and destroyed shacks. As the men dug in for the night, Desmond noticed one of the odd-looking tombs within the company perimeter and entered it. It was dark and damp and permeated with a heavy, sweetish odor.

Several large earthen urns stood in the back of the cavern; Desmond peered into one. In the dim light he saw a skeleton. Desmond figured that this would be the last place a Japanese would enter. He bedded down in the tomb for the night. Darkness had hardly settled, however, before he realized he had made a whopping big mistake. He was alone and unarmed. If the Japanese came in, he was helpless. What was worse, he couldn't leave. If he came crawling out of that tomb at night he'd be shot to pieces by his own men. It was a long night, and, as Desmond ruefully admitted to his buddies next morning, he did more praying than sleeping.

Before the soldiers advanced to their positions next morning, Captain Vernon pointed out the terrain to the company. The bivouac area was on a small ridge, looking to the south. The American forces had cut the island in two and were working southward. The major Japanese fortifications and forces occupied the rugged limestone hills of the southern part of the island.

Across the littered valley rose another brown rocky ridge, known as the Maeda Escarpment. Its slopes rose sharply from the valley, covered with huge boulders. At the top of the slope stood a sheer rock cliff, from 30 to 50 feet high. Maeda Escarpment commanded the entire width of the island. From it the Japanese could see the activities of the advancing forces from sea to sea and for many miles back. It had to be taken.

"On top of that hill and behind it," Captain Vernon told the men, "the enemy has built a complex of pillboxes, fortifications, and emplacements. Two divisions have been cut to pieces trying to take that hill. Now it's up to us. We will move up and take our position at the bottom of the cliff. From there we will study the situation and make our plans."

The men looked around at each other. Company B had undertaken some dangerous missions, but nothing like this. Several of the men looked at Desmond. He tried to appear calm and reassuring. He knew his importance to their morale. A good medic could mean the difference between life and death, and Desmond Doss had proved himself to be a good medic, over and over.

In the early morning, under cover of darkness, the company moved into its new position at the base of the cliff. There were big rocks piled together, making crevices, covering caves. Under the protection of the cliff the company area seemed fairly safe.

That afternoon Lieutenant Gornto and Sergeant Potts explored the cliff, and determined where it could be scaled. They cautiously climbed it and, keeping low, peered out across the hill. They identified several concrete-and-steel pillboxes and emplacements. They sent back to battalion headquarters for rope, a large supply of demolition equipment, and flame-throwers. Next day they'd attack the escarpment.

At daybreak Potts and Edgette had their squads ready. Desmond was with them. He knew they wanted him along. He was scared, but he was also curious. He had a captured pair of Japanese binoculars, and he hung them around his neck. If the view from the escarpment was so great, he wanted to see it!

One by one, laboriously, they scaled the cliff. At the top, keeping prone, creeping on their bellies, they collected loose rocks—there were hundreds of them—pushed them forward, and built a kind of rock wall a few feet back from the edge of the cliff for protection. They secured one end of the rope to a boulder and dropped the other end over the cliff, for reinforcements. Another squad climbed up this way. It was easier going. By keeping low, presenting little target, the small force managed to avoid drawing enemy small-arms fire. There was no work for Desmond, and he squirmed around to face northward. The military importance of the escarpment immediately became apparent. He could see every phase of American military activity to the rear. Out to sea he saw transports at anchor and landing craft bringing supplies. A geyser of seawater went up near one as a Japanese shell exploded. They were sitting ducks.

Whump! The sound of an explosion came from the other side of the low rock wall. Another, and another, this time from behind them at the base of the cliff. Desmond had heard that sound before.

"Mortars!" he shouted. "Knee mortars!"

Knee mortars could be fired at such an angle of elevation that they could drop almost straight down. The little rock wall furnished no protection against a mortar attack. The Japanese were zeroing in; it was only a matter of minutes.

"Pull back," the word was passed. "Get back down the cliff."

Captain Vernon sent word of the withdrawal back to Battalion, and received orders to continue the attack the next day. Company A would also attack, higher on the escarpment, to the left. Three large cargo nets, the kind thrown over the side of the ship for debarkation purposes, were sent out from Battalion. Pieces of timber were used to thread the three together into one large net.

As dawn approached, Lieutenant Gornto called Doss to him. "You were pretty good with knots back in mountain training," Gornto recalled. "How about helping us secure these nets to the top of the cliff?"

"Yes, sir," Doss said. He and a couple of other men, lines secured to their belts, climbed the cliff. Keeping low, Desmond secured the end of his rope to a large boulder. Then they pulled up the net and made it fast. The entire platoon could now swarm the cliff almost in a body. Preparations complete, Desmond and the other men climbed back down the nets.

Gornto would lead the assault. The major objective was a huge pillbox several yards back from the edge of the cliff. It was from this fortified vantage point that the Japanese were able to call down that dangerous mortar fire. Gornto assembled a squad of the toughest veterans, beginning with the three sergeants, Potts, Edgette, and O'Connell. Desmond volunteered.

"This is going to be a dangerous mission, Doss," Gornto told him. "You don't have to go."

"I feel I should, lieutenant," Desmond said. "I may be needed. But, lieutenant, I'd like to ask a favor before we go."

"OK, Doss, what is it?" Gornto said.

"Sir, I believe that prayer is the biggest lifesaver there is. I believe that every man should have a word of prayer before he puts his foot on the rope ladder to go up that cliff."

What Desmond meant was that each man should have the opportunity to say a silent prayer himself. Gornto, however, called the group of men together and told them that Doss was going to lead them in prayer. Desmond had not thought about making a formal prayer, but he did not let his lack of preparation delay him. He stepped forward and said the first words that came into his heart.

"Our heavenly Father," Desmond prayed, "please give our lieutenant wisdom and understanding so that he can give us the right orders, because our lives will be in his charge. Please give each and every one of us the wisdom and understanding concerning how to take all the safety precautions necessary in order that, if it be Thy will, oh, Lord, we may all come back alive. And further we ask that if there be any here who are not prepared to meet their Maker, they prepare themselves now through prayer before they climb the cliff. We ask all this in Jesus' name."

For another moment the war on the escarpment stood still as the men remained motionless. Desmond was positive that all were praying, even those who had never prayed before. Then, confident, almost carefree, they turned to the cargo net at the bottom of the cliff, signaling to Company A to the west that they were beginning the assault. The members of the suicide squad, with their medic at their heels, climbed the cliff and without hesitation moved on across the top of the hill toward the enemy pillbox.

Two tanks, a thousand yards back, poured in a coordinated fire on the pillbox. It was ineffective. Now Gornto beckoned Pfc Norman Black to come up with his bazooka. Black fired several times. The explosions uncovered an aperture in the side of the concrete dome. Under cover of two automatic riflemen from the flanks, one of the men ran forward and threw a satchel charge of explosives into the pillbox. Heavy logs which had obviously formed a part of the fortification flew up like matchsticks. A soldier rushed to it with a flamethrower and directed its full force into the gaping hole.

No more resistance came from it, and the entire assault squad moved forward. They saw only a large hole; the sides had caved in, covering whatever openings had been there before.

Covered by a light machine gun mounted on the pillbox, Gornto's squad moved out over the hilltop. They blew up several other pillboxes in the immediate area. Now the Japanese behind the edge of the hill began throwing hand grenades on the advancing Americans. The forward men in the squad threw grenades back. A furious battle ensued.

Desmond was making himself small in a hole behind the rock wall. The forward men ran out of grenades and cried for more to be passed up. A box of grenades suddenly appeared at the top of the cliff.

"Pass 'em on," the soldier who had carried them up said. Desmond looked over the wall. The next man was several feet away. If he came back, crawled over the little wall, picked up the grenades and returned, he'd be an easy target coming and going. It would be his life, and the men forward would not have their grenades. It would be their lives too.

Desmond picked up the grenades and passed them over the wall. It was the first and only time he touched a lethal weapon.

In the meantime Company A had failed to take its assigned position. The first five men to reach the top of the cliff had been killed instantly.

But the Company B assault squad had secured a large area on the top of the escarpment. Gornto and Desmond looked around for any wounded who might need attention, and also for the dead. But there were none. In all this furious action the squad from Company B had had just one injury. Sergeant O'Connell's hand had been hit by a piece of flying rock!

This was incredible—to everyone except Desmond. Had he not prayed?

Captain Vernon sent the third platoon up on the escarpment to relieve the assault squad. Desmond stayed on top. He sensed that he would be needed, and he was. The end had come to that miraculous period in which a large group of men operated under a hail of Japanese bullets and hand grenades with no serious wound. It was as though Desmond's prayer had specifically covered one group of men for one period of time. Now that group had retired to safety, and the time was over. The cry "Medic" went up again and again, and Desmond crawled all over the hilltop ministering to the wounded. Then he would help them to the edge of the cliff and down the cargo net.

Night came, but it brought no peace, no quiet. Japanese artillery and mortar fire increased. After midnight a large group of Japanese rushed the men on the escarpment, throwing grenades, then joining in hand-to-hand combat. The Americans were forced down off the escarpment. And in the meantime, Japanese suddenly began appearing beneath the cliff. They oozed out of holes and crevices. For the first time the company realized that the honeycombing of the hill extended out into their own area. The enemy was underneath them!

When dawn broke after a wild night, Desmond Doss had gone to the aid of eighteen men, including Potts and Edgette. Lieutenant Brister was in shock. Four of the eighteen men were dead. One of them was a company aid man who had just come in as a replacement. During the night he had reached out of his hole for his canteen and was shot through the head.

But as soon as dawn broke, Captain Vernon had his men moving forward again to recapture what they had lost during the night. Again

Desmond was with them. One episode followed another. A lieutenant was leading three men in a running attack on an emplacement. The lieutenant drew back his hand to throw a grenade. A bullet hit him, delayed the throw. The grenade went off, taking his hand with it, and wounding the other three men. It all happened right in front of Doss. In a swift second, he had four men to take care of there on the bullet-swept hilltop.

He fell to his knees among them. Men behind him were throwing grenades over his head into the Japanese lines. They saw Desmond, and the word passed up and down the line to be careful. The grenades stopped coming. The Japanese began peering over the hillside to see what caused the cessation.

"Don't stop now!" Desmond shouted back to his men. "Keep 'em coming!"

The fellows started throwing grenades over his head again and to either side, keeping the Japanese down so he could finish the job. He had to stanch the flow of blood from the lieutenant's stump as well as from other wounds, and put dressings on the wounds of the three other men. Two of them could crawl, and Desmond sent them back on their own. He grabbed the lieutenant by the collar and hunched him, a few inches at a time, back toward the edge of the cliff. An infantryman ran up and helped the fourth soldier get back to his lines.

A little later Desmond was crouched on the hillside watching a fellow soldier attack the mouth of a Japanese-held cave. The man fired several shots into the cave, then took his satchel charge and started to heave it in. Just as it left his hand a bullet struck him. As Desmond watched, he saw the man's teeth fly out.

"Cover me!" Desmond shouted to a pair of infantry men inching their way forward behind him. As they fired into the cave, Desmond ran to the wounded man, ripped open his shirt, located a hole in his chest through which the blood was pouring, and slapped a heavy dressing on it. The soldier was unconscious, but Desmond raised him up and got his arm over his shoulder. Clutching the wounded man's arm with one hand, holding onto his waist with the other, Desmond ran toward his own lines, dragging the wounded man with him. They reached the edge of the cliff. But it had been a needless mission. The soldier was dead.

"Medic, medic!" came the shout. Desmond had no time to mourn. A shell had fallen in a machine gun emplacement far up the hill to the left.

Desmond, stooped low, zigzagging, ran to the spot. Little was left of one of the men, just a disembodied hand still clutching the machine gun. The shell had blown the lower leg off the other man. His thigh was already swelling. Desmond bound it tightly, then began dragging the machine gunner toward the nearest point at the top of the cliff. A deep ravine cut through his path. A wooden ladder leaned against the side of the ravine. Desmond pulled it up and extended it across to the other bank of the ravine; it just reached.

A rifleman was watching from a shell hole. "Help me!" Desmond said in a voice that was half plea, half command. The soldier came to his aid. Desmond backed out on the ladder, dragging the wounded man's head and shoulders. The soldier followed, helping as best he could. The ladder was old and rickety. It had been spliced in two places. It bent and creaked, but Desmond kept going, and his helper followed. The ladder held, and they got the man to safety.

Day followed day, and still the fighting continued. The nights were as bad. Up on the escarpment the Japanese kept up a constant grenade barrage and continued to infiltrate. Below, at the base of the cliff, it was even more dangerous. Men would find a crevice in the rocks, crawl into it, barricade the front, and sink into a coma of exhaustion. From behind them Japanese would silently sneak out of a hole in the rear of the crevice and slit the Americans' throats while they slept.

But an even greater danger was the endless barrage of mortar shells. In some places along the cliff the base was eroded away, and the overhang furnished excellent protection. In front of one of these places rocks had been piled up to furnish additional defense.

One night Desmond shared this cavern-like refuge with a rifleman in the 2d Platoon. He noticed a large hole in the back of the crevice, but it seemed to go nowhere. Nevertheless, they decided it would be wise for one to stay awake while the other slept, two hours on and two off. Desmond took guard first, sitting back near the edge of the hole. After a few minutes he heard a rustling noise, then someone whispering. The sounds came from the hole—and the whispering was in Japanese! He awakened the soldier with whom he shared the hole and whispered to him to listen.

"Uh huh," the soldier mumbled, and resumed snoring. Desmond lay awake, hardly daring to breathe himself, listening to the mysterious sounds coming from the unseen enemy just a few feet away.

When it was time for the rifleman to take his turn on watch, Desmond woke him again. Within five minutes the fellow was snoring. And again the ominous rustlings came from beneath.

All night Desmond tried to get his partner to pull his turn at guard. He would promise to do so, but would not stay awake two minutes. Desmond tried to get him to change places with him. At least then, if the Japanese came out of the hole, they'd find the sleeping guard first. But though almost comatose, the soldier was too smart to change positions.

The sleeping soldier had two hand grenades. Just one, dropped down that hole, would put an end to the danger, and Desmond could go to sleep himself. That night was the closest Desmond ever came to taking life, for he considered dropping those grenades. But he put the idea out of his mind. Though it could well become a matter of life or death for himself, Desmond would not break the sixth commandment.

And so he stayed awake the entire night. During that night he came to one firm conclusion: If he lived through it, God willing, he'd never spend another night either in that hole or with that soldier.

The next night he kept both those resolutions, holing up with Gornto in a protected place serving as the platoon command post. Just before dawn Desmond heard the familiar cry, "Medic, medic!" Intuition told him what had happened.

"You don't have to go, Doss," Lieutenant Gornto said, but Desmond felt he had no choice.

"Pass the word along that I'm coming, so they won't shoot me," he said. Feeling his way in the dark, whispering reassuringly in the hill-country accent no Japanese could mimic, to calm itchy trigger fingers, he proceeded to the cave where he had spent the previous wakeful night.

Inside was one soldier. Another lay several feet away. Both were torn and bleeding, victims of grenades. Probably the grenades had come from the hole where he had heard the Japanese whispering the night before. Desmond used up all his large battle dressings on the wounded men and sent them back to the aid station at daybreak. But he did not believe they could survive.

The escarpment continued to hold up the entire American advance. Higher commands from division headquarters to the Pentagon were concerned about the Japanese resistance on that honeycombed hill. Press dispatches told the entire nation about the battle raging there. Of particular interest was the account of the first day's battle in which no one had been seriously injured, no one killed. Such operations just don't happen. A Signal Corps photographer came to the company CP two or three days after Gornto had led the assault squad up the cliff.

"I understand you had a fantastic operation here," the photographer said, "blowing a dozen pillboxes and not having one man killed."

"That's right." Captain Vernon explained the situation. The Signal Corps photographer looked at the cargo nets.

"We'll send somebody up with you so you can get pictures from on top," Captain Vernon volunteered.

"Oh, no," the photographer said quickly. "I can take the pictures from down here."

It was Desmond Doss and Jim Dorris who climbed up the cargo net and stood at the top of the cliff, for the photographer's benefit.

"C'mon up," Desmond called. He and Dorris were fairly well concealed by the natural slope and the rock wall that had been built the first day.

But the photographer did not appreciate the invitation. "I haven't lost anything up there," he explained.

Fighting on the fire-swept escarpment by day, prey of the enemy slipping out of caves by night, even seasoned veterans began to show fear. All around him Desmond saw the drawn faces, the staring eyes, the twitching hands of extreme mental strain. One of the top noncoms of the company sought out Desmond and told him, "I can't go on any longer. My luck's run out. You can say I'm sick. You got to send me back."

Doss shook his head. He understood the man's fears, but he could not approve. "There's nothing the matter with you," he said. "Stop talking like that. Pull yourself together and you'll be all right."

He later heard that the sergeant was going around offering to pay other soldiers to shoot him in the leg or arm.

On the other hand, a corporal, one of the original members of the company and a man who had given his best from the first day he had joined the outfit, came down with some ailment which resulted in a high fever and swollen glands. His entire neck was swollen, red and painful to the touch. He couldn't turn his head; he had to move his entire body to look to the side. With such pain, and under such a handicap, he could not possibly take care of himself on the escarpment. Desmond sent him back to the battalion aid station. A few hours later, here came the corporal back again. The medical officer at the aid station had told him to go back to duty and "take it easy."

"How can you take it easy up here?" Desmond demanded. He was actually angry. "You go back to battalion aid station, and you tell them that I said you are in no fit condition to be up here. If the doctor wants to see me about it, I'll come back and talk to him. But don't you come back up here. You understand?"

The little corporal with the swollen neck started the long trip back to the battalion aid station again. Desmond watched him go. "That's a good man with not one cowardly drop of blood in his entire body," he fumed for the benefit of anyone who would listen. "I won't let them send him back up here to get killed."

The dead lay everywhere. On top of the escarpment both Americans and Japanese lay where they had fallen. Down below, the American dead were removed, but nobody took the time to pick up the enemy bodies. A Japanese officer who had infiltrated the company area and killed two of Desmond's buddies before being killed himself lay sprawled over a rock. His dead hand still clutched his saber. That saber would have brought $100 from the souvenir hunters in the rear echelons or the Navy, but none of the men up front even looked at it.

But all this death had to have some effect. Desmond worried more about the buddies he was losing every day than about himself. One day, moving like a sleepwalker, he went through the GI ritual of pouring some gasoline into a tin can, then throwing in a match to make a quick fire to heat his food. He sat on his heels and watched the flame. He felt moisture on his cheeks and brushed it away with his knuckles. For the first time he realized that he was crying. Then he looked at the fire that he had just built.

"Why am I doing this?" he asked himself. *"I'm not hungry!"*

He realized that he had to pull himself together, stop thinking about his good friends who had been killed—too many of them—and replace his trust in the Lord.

The fighting for the escarpment continued day after bloody day, night after fearful night. Though the enemy had been pretty well cleared off the top of the hill, an area about as wide as a football field, the slope on the other side was dotted with pillboxes leading to the maze of tunnels beneath. By day the Americans occupied the top of the hill, attempting to push forward. By night the Japanese crept out of their holes and slithered soundlessly over the terrain.

A key Japanese emplacement, really just a fortified gaping entrance to the tunnels beneath, was spotted just over the lip of the far slope of the escarpment. The Americans tried to hit it with mortars and artillery, but it was protected by the slope of the hill. Repeated efforts were made to knock it out. Sergeant John Maholic, the popular noncom from the heavy weapons platoon, got close enough to throw a grenade in. The Japanese threw it right back out again. Under cover of friendly fire two engineers ran forward and dumped in a satchel charge. The Japanese pulled the fuses before it could explode.

Someone at headquarters got the brilliant idea of fashioning a trough out of tin to run all across the hill. Gasoline poured into the trough at the American side would flow across into the Japanese hole. Then a grenade thrown in would ignite it. But laying the trough was a clumsy operation, and there wasn't enough elevation for the gas to flow. Japanese continued to emerge from the hole.

"I'm going to blast that hole if it kills me," Sergeant Maholic said. He led a squad of volunteers across the top of the escarpment to the lip of the hill. As his men covered him, he jumped up and ran toward the hole, a grenade in each hand.

Bullets thudded into the sergeant's body as he ran. He staggered, then fell. His momentum carried him almost to the edge of the hole. He lay there, still. The grenades rolled on and exploded harmlessly.

"Maholic's hit!" the word got back to Doss. He was helping a wounded man on top of the escarpment. Though it was almost certain that Maholic was dead and Desmond was numb with exhaustion, he went forward without hesitation. He knew the respect the men had for Maholic. A man from his squad accompanied Doss, and together they crawled almost to the very lip of the hole. They grabbed Maholic's feet and dragged his body back up the hill and to the cover of a shell hole. There Desmond examined him. John Maholic was dead. From the nature of his wounds, he had probably died instantly.

Word swept through the company, and was taken back to the battalion headquarters by the wounded: Desmond Doss, who had risked his life so many times to save the wounded, had done it again for a dead man.

That afternoon Desmond had to go back to the battalion aid station to pick up supplies. Captain Tann greeted him with, of all things, an admonition.

"What's this I hear about you risking your neck to save a dead man?" he railed. "You'll only succeed in getting yourself killed that way, and dead medics are no good to anybody. If I ever hear of you doing anything like that again, I'll pull you back."

But even as he talked his voice softened. Desmond Doss looked as if he had been fighting a war all by himself. His face was drawn. He was edgy and irritable. His hands trembled. His uniform was brown with the blood of men he had treated and dragged to safety, and with his own blood, for a flying rock had cut a nasty gash.

The day was ending. "You're going to spend the night here, Doss," Captain Tann told him.

"Oh, no, captain, I'd better get back to the company," Desmond said.

"You'll stay here and that's an order," Tann said. "We're going to feed you and see to it that you get some sleep. I don't even want you to pull any guard duty."

After chow the captain directed Desmond to a quiet cave. An underground stream bubbled with a soothing sound. After his nightly prayers Desmond opened up a litter and stretched out on it. Before he could really appreciate the security, the quiet, and the soft murmur of the brook, he was sound asleep.

In the morning, refreshed after his first full night's sleep since going up to the escarpment, Desmond realized how close he had been to complete exhaustion, both physical and mental.

Before he left the aid station, litter bearers brought in a lieutenant from another company. He was a young officer, and he was worried that all of his men were going to be killed in a forthcoming attack.

"I've got to get to them; I've got to get to them!" he kept crying. "Don't you understand? Help me get to my men!" His eyes were bloodshot, his nose running, his face contorted. He kept trying to get off the litter, but he was in such an hysterical state that he could barely move his arms. When Desmond last saw him, he was lying there weeping helplessly.

"That almost happened to me," Desmond thought, and resolved again, with the help of God, to keep his nerves under control.

It was another rough day on the escarpment. Dorris was wounded; now Desmond was the only medic for the entire company. He holed up that night with Gornto and five of his riflemen. Surely this would be a large enough force both to enable him to get some rest between standing guard duty and to guarantee protection against enemy soldiers infiltrating the company area. They had found an indentation in the side of the cliff against which a flat rock leaned, and had piled up fired mortar shells filled with rocks to close in one side. A rock parapet stood on the other side.

Desmond pulled guard first. Nearby a mortar squad was firing, keeping the Japanese from moving around on top of the escarpment. After several *whumps,* he heard a different sound, the explosion of a grenade. Desmond saw, standing on the parapet outside, outlined against the sky, a Japanese soldier.

"Lieutenant!" he whispered, and pointed the soldier out to Gornto.

"We'll get him," Gornto said. But firing from the darkness through the narrow aperture was difficult. The bullets missed. But the Japanese saw the flashes. He began trying to throw grenades through the opening. It was just a question of time before he'd get one in and wipe out all seven of them. The men inside were trapped. Desmond realized that this time death was inevitable. He started to pray for Gornto and the other men as well as for himself.

And the Lord heard his prayer. Gornto had left his pack outside the cave. In it were two white phosphorus grenades. The next grenade flung by the Japanese landed on that pack. Somehow, instead of exploding, the phosphorus grenades merely burned. A great cloud of white smoke resulted. The wind was just right, and blew it over the enemy soldier. He couldn't take it.

"Let's get out of here!" Gornto hollered. One after the other they squeezed through the narrow aperture. Desmond, handicapped by his aid kits, had to let the others go first. The billowing clouds of smoke had almost dissipated by the time he got out of the cavern.

Running hard in the darkness, he was on Gornto's heels. Suddenly the shadowy silhouette of the lieutenant became two silhouettes. The Japanese had stepped out to block his path. Desmond piled into the two scuffling forms, and bounced off to the side. He felt himself falling. He'd gone over the edge of the parapet. He and his equipment hit bottom with a thud. An agonizing pain shot through his left leg. It would not bear his weight.

But he couldn't stay there. The ammunition dump was nearby, with sentries posted. Dragging his leg behind him, announcing his identity in hoarse whispers, Desmond crawled to the dump, found a hole, and burrowed in. Feeling his leg with his fingers in the dark, he found that it was bleeding badly, and placed dressings on it to stop the blood. He could do nothing further, so he went back to sleep.

Dawn came. Desmond knew he should evacuate himself and his bad leg back to the battalion aid station. He could do his wounded buddies no good up here if his leg would not permit him to get to them. Yet he did not go. He was the only medic left, not just of Company B, but of the entire force at the escarpment. A medic with only one leg was better than no medic at all.

It was Saturday, May 5, the Sabbath. Breakfast over, he took his Bible and lesson pamphlet out of his pack and sat down, his back against a rock. For just a moment he allowed his thoughts to dwell on Dorothy, his parents, and his friends back home, going to church on a peaceful Sabbath far from the sounds of war. He did not envy them. By being here in this terrible place, he knew, he was doing his share to make it possible for them, and all Americans, to continue worshiping their God according to their own beliefs as a part of their heritage. He opened his lesson and began to read.

"How are things up on the hill?" The voice came from a full colonel standing above him. Desmond started to scramble to his feet, bad leg and all, but the colonel motioned him to stay where he was.

"I haven't been up there this morning, sir," Desmond said. "Our company CP is right over there, and you can check with them!"

The colonel nodded. "I want to see how our artillery is doing," he said, and proceeded on to the cargo nets.

Desmond turned back to his lesson. Several minutes went by. Then, from the top of the cliff, came the familiar cry, "Medic, medic!"

Desmond looked up at the men calling him. It was the Sabbath, and he had only one good leg. Nevertheless he answered, "What's the matter?"

"That colonel, the artillery spotter, he's been hit bad," the men shouted down.

Without thinking, Desmond grabbed his aid kits, jumped up, and started toward the cliff. His weight fell on his bad leg and it buckled under him. He went down, hard. Someone gave him a hand up.

"Oh, Lord, please help me," Desmond murmured. Again he put his weight on his bad leg. It held. One step, two, and then he realized that his bruised and wrenched leg was not paining him a bit. With his aid kits slung over his shoulders, he climbed the net to the top of the cliff, then carefully made his way toward the shell hole where the injured colonel lay.

Bullets whined over his head, and mortars and artillery shells burst on the hill. He paid no attention. By now he was used to the sound of death. He reached the shell hole and jumped in with the injured, unconscious colonel. A piece of shrapnel from a shell burst had shattered his arm and then ripped its way right on through his chest and back. He was bleeding heavily, and breathing through the hole in his chest. Desmond shouted to a man in the nearest shell hole to pass the word back that he needed blood plasma, and quick. He selected his largest battle dressings and tied them over the two large holes, front and back, to stop the gush of blood and the chest breathing.

He had finished the bandaging job when a soldier slid feet first into the hole with him. He had brought the blood plasma. Desmond inserted the large transfusion needle into a vein in the colonel's arm. In order for the plasma to drain from the container into the vein, it was necessary to hold it high. This meant exposing himself to the enemy just over the hill. Motionless, feeling naked, Desmond knelt there in full view of two armies, letting the life-giving plasma flow into the wounded man's vein. From behind, his men shouted at him to get down and fired across him to give him protection.

Another man skidded in with a litter. As Desmond held the container of plasma, the two men in the hole with him opened up the litter and eased the limp form onto it. The trip back toward the edge of the cliff, running, bent over, carrying the colonel, was a rough haul. The surgical dressings had slipped and the bleeding had commenced again. Desmond tied the dressings back. The transfusion needle had slipped out of the vein. Desmond tried to get it back in, but the vein had collapsed. He sent word to the battalion aid station that he had a colonel in serious condition and needed help. Captain Tann and Sergeant Howell appeared, but they were not able to get the needle back into the collapsed vein either.

"I think we'd better get him back to the hospital," Tann said. "We're not doing him any good here."

Four men picked up the litter and started carrying the colonel back toward the aid station. He died before he got there.

Desmond returned to his Sabbath School lesson. Again he was interrupted, this time by Captain Vernon.

"Doss," the captain said, "we have orders to move across the hill and take that pillbox no matter what the cost. Lieutenant Phillips is leading the attack. I know it is your Sabbath, and I know you don't have to go on this mission. But the men would like to have you with them and so would I."

"I'll go, captain," Doss said without hesitation. His Saviour had treated men on the Sabbath, and he could do no less. "But I'd like to finish my Sabbath School lesson first."

Captain Vernon opened his mouth to speak, then closed it again. He studied his company aid man for a moment. Doss's cotton uniform was dark brown and stiff with dried blood, the blood of the men whose lives he had saved and attempted to save. His eyes were sunk deep in their sockets with exhaustion. Vernon knew that he had seriously injured his leg and had nevertheless just gone out under fire to do his best to save a wounded man. How many men had Doss saved since this bloody battle had begun? The captain could not count them.

Vernon nodded agreement. "We'll wait for you."

Captain Vernon did not tell his company aid man that orders for this special mission had come down from 10th Army to Corps to Division to Regiment to Battalion to Company B. The entire American advance in Okinawa, a line several miles across and involving several divisions, was being held up by this one strong position. From the escarpment the Japanese dominated the terrain on either side. It could truly be said that the success of the Okinawa campaign rested on this mission.

And Captain Vernon delayed it so that one tired Sabbath keeper could read his Bible.

Not knowing he was holding up a war, Desmond reached the conclusion of the lesson. He closed his Bible, bowed his head and finished with a prayer. He stood up. Again his bruised leg miraculously supported him. "I'm ready when you are, captain."

The entire 1st Battalion was in on the attack, although Company B was to spearhead it. The company had been built up to well over 200 men for the Okinawa campaign, but after a week on the escarpment its fighting strength was down to 155 men.

These men were going into an even bigger battle than their worst fears, far bigger than the generals and their intelligence experts realized. None of them had any way of knowing that the entire Japanese strategy was keyed on this day. In every island battle prior to Okinawa, the Japanese had contested the Americans on the beachhead. This time their strategy was different. It was to permit the Americans to come onto Okinawa, all six divisions of them, unopposed. When the entire American force was on shore, a swarm of Kamikazes would be unleashed to sink the American fleet and cut off the supply lines. That would leave the forces stranded on the island.

The second step in their strategy was to wipe out those forces. The place chosen: A line anchored on the Maeda Escarpment, the most favorable terrain on the island for a counterattack. The time, that very day, May 5.

The first part of the program had failed; the Kamikazes had proved to be only a nuisance. But the second phase, the counterattack, was scheduled to go on nonetheless.

The high commands of two great forces, many miles apart, had chosen this very day to attack. Their point of contact was the escarpment. As the Japanese waited in their holes for zero hour, the Americans were beginning their advance. In the center was the 77th Division. At the apex of its attacking wedge the 307th Regiment, the First Battalion, Company B, and finally Lieutenant Phillips and his handpicked group of five volunteers. Their mission: The final assault on the big pillbox on the reverse slope of the hill.

The six men, covered by sweeping fire from the rear, crossed the broad top of the hill and crawled down the reverse slope toward the big hole. Each man carried a five-gallon can of gasoline. At Phillips's signal they removed the caps and tossed the cans in the hole. Phillips waited a moment, then tossed in a white phosphorus grenade. There was silence for a moment, then a mighty rumble. The entire hill shook.

Phillips and his men held on tight and looked at each other in wonder. This was more than they had expected. Far down beneath them an ammunition dump had obviously gone off. A few moments later the officers observing from the hills far to the rear across the valley and from the planes overhead saw a strange phenomenon. Puffs of white smoke came out of a hundred holes and crevices on top of the hill and from the slopes on all sides.

And out of many of those holes, even those on the American side, poured Japanese soldiers. They came running, screaming, firing rifles, and throwing grenades. This was the counterattack on which the Japanese pinned all their hopes. The whole thing reminded Desmond of hitting a hornet's nest with a stick, and seeing it erupt. The Americans met them head on. Captain Vernon brought every man up on the escarpment and the force dug in and held. But then the sheer weight of numbers and firepower, both from in front and from the rear, proved overwhelming.

At first there was the semblance of an orderly retreat, but then panic set in. Officers and noncoms were ranging up and down the hill shouting, threatening, trying to keep the men falling back in an orderly fashion. Some of the noncoms pointed their guns at their men, threatening to shoot anyone who fled. But panic and hysteria swept over the hilltop and the entire battalion, or what was left of it, began running back toward the cliff. Those men hit by enemy bullets and shells were left to lie where they had fallen, whether wounded or dead.

In the midst of this mad rush was the one remaining medic in the whole battalion, Desmond Doss. He ran from one fallen man to the other doing what he could. He didn't think of saving his own skin; he was too busy. He didn't think about the Japanese soldiers on the hilltop with him, shooting and throwing grenades. God had looked after him before. Why would He stop now? Trained as a medical soldier, seasoned by a hundred actions, secure in his conviction that when he was aiding his fellow men God was looking after him, Desmond Doss went calmly about his business of aiding the wounded, the only sane man on a hilltop mad with murder and fear.

Some of the other men, seeing him going about his business, were shamed into halting their pell-mell rush to the rear. Some gave him a hand with the wounded, helping them, dragging them to the edge of the cliff. But for hours it seemed to Desmond as though he was up there alone on top of the escarpment, raked by enemy fire, treating the wounded, pulling them back to the edge, then going back for more.

Those men who had been able to make their way down the cargo nets had collapsed and lay panting, regathering their breath and their senses. How long they had been there nobody really knew, when one of them happened to look up to the top of the cliff. He saw Desmond Doss standing there alone, the last unwounded man. The next thing the men at the bottom of the cliff knew, a litter with a wounded soldier strapped on it was being slowly lowered down the face of the cliff. Desmond had tied the man on it, had then taken a turn of the rope around the shattered stump of a tree, and was slowly paying out rope to permit the litter and its human burden to descend. A few feet from the bottom the rope securing the soldier to the litter slipped, and the unconscious man almost fell off. But a couple of men ran forward to steady the litter.

"Take him off!" Doss shouted down to them from above. "I've got more men up here. Send this one straight back to the aid station. Nonstop! He's bad off."

The men at the bottom untied the litter and removed the wounded man. They started to tie the litter back on to the rope, but Desmond stopped them.

"I don't want it," he called down. He had seen that first man nearly slip off and somehow, amidst all the confusion, his memory produced a picture in his mind. He remembered how he had tied a bowline in a double length of rope during mountain-climbing in West Virginia. Now he doubled the end of the rope and tied that bowline. The result was two loops, two loops that would not slip.

The area at the top of the cliff was covered with wounded men, conscious and unconscious. Desmond chose one of the men who seemed to be the most seriously injured. He slipped one of the man's legs through one of the loops of his bowline, the other leg through the other loop. Then he passed the rope around the man's chest and tied another bowline there. Now, holding on to the end of the rope, he gently rolled the wounded man over the edge of the cliff and, using the friction of the loop around the tree as a brake, let him down to the ground beneath.

"That man's seriously injured," he called down. "Get him back to the aid station nonstop!"

In that way, working alone, the only able-bodied man on the entire hilltop, Desmond lowered one man after another to safety and treatment beneath. He was partially protected by the slope and the rock wall, but as it was necessary for him to remain standing during several steps of the complete procedure, his head and shoulders were often exposed. Why did not Japanese bullets seek him out? Again Desmond accepted it as the beneficent will of his God.

Why did the Japanese, who had already chased the Americans back across the hilltop, not follow up their advantage? Only they knew. Perhaps the underground explosion had wreaked too great a toll for them to be able to mount their planned counterattack. Perhaps the artillery and mortar fire that Vernon called down on the top was sufficiently effective.

At any rate, Desmond remained on top of the cliff until he had lowered every wounded man to safety. How many men were there? No one counted. Only after it was all over and the full immensity of his actions began to sink in through the minds of the men who had witnessed it, did anyone begin to estimate the number. Captain Vernon and Lieutenant Gornto recalled that a total of 155 men had taken part in the abortive assault. They took a quick head count; only fifty-five men were on their feet at the base of the cliff. The difference—100 men—was the number they credited Desmond with saving.

He protested. "There couldn't have been more than fifty. It would have been impossible for me to handle any more than that."

"We'll split the difference with you," Captain Vernon proposed. "The official record will state seventy-five men saved by Pfc Doss."

Frightening and costly as the Japanese counterattack had been, it marked the last action on the escarpment. When the Japanese did not follow up their advantage, the Americans went back up on the hill and this time they stayed. The next day Company B, or what was left of it, was replaced with a fresh unit. Doss went back with them, tired to the very marrow of his bones.

Again Captain Tann and Sergeant Howell welcomed him. Tann looked at Desmond's uniform and shuddered. It was completely stiff and brown with dried blood and covered with flies.

"We're going to get you a new uniform," he promised.

Armies do not carry such luxuries as clean uniforms, even for such bloody campaigns as Okinawa; cargo space is taken up by such essentials as ammunition and food. But somehow fresh fatigues were found for the medic who had saved seventy-five men in one action. Desmond went back to the supply depot to get them. He scrubbed from the skin out, shaved, then put on his new uniform. If he'd had on a full-dress uniform he couldn't have been more impressive. An army photographer was rounded up to take a picture of a company aid man in a new uniform.

The commanding officer of the division, Major General A. D. Bruce, had heard of Desmond's heroism and wanted to talk to him personally. He came all the way up to the battalion aid station to see him. That was when Desmond was getting his new uniform.

Next day Desmond received an even greater present. It was a huge package from the States. Over the years Desmond had always listened to the Adventist radio program, *The Voice of Prophecy*. He had contributed to it for a long time. Following the Leyte campaign, in gratitude to the Almighty for sparing him during that bloody operation, Desmond sent in another contribution to *The Voice of Prophecy*. In this communication he asked Elder H. M. S. Richards, the Adventist evangelist who conducted the program, to send him some books for distribution among the company.

And now the books had arrived. Desmond got a big thrill out of unpacking them, passing them around to the men of the company. The number worked out perfectly. There was one book for every man, and one left over. The largest book was *The Great Controversy*, perhaps the most famous volume in the Adventist library, and Desmond presented it to the entire company to be kept in the field desk.

It was a fitting end to the battle of the escarpment. There was talk of another decoration to go with the Bronze Star he had won on Leyte. The officers wanted to recommend him for two Purple Hearts, one for the gash caused by the ricocheting rock, one for the injured leg. Although many a Purple Heart has been given for less, Desmond said one to cover both actions would be enough.

More important than a medal was the knowledge that he had been able to take care of the men he loved and send many of them back to their families.

It had been a busy Sabbath!

CHAPTER 5

THE LAST PATROL

After just two weeks of rest, Company B, with ninety-three replacements and several of the old men back after recovering from minor wounds and shock, returned to action. The few men who had been with it from the beginning might well have thought that by now they had seen everything. Yet a completely new type of action had been assigned them.

Captain Vernon took his key men, including Desmond, to the top of the hill known as Chocolate Drop, a mile or two past the escarpment, and pointed out the next hill. This would be their objective. Vernon's finger traced in the intervening valley a series of towers for a power line leading to the objective. Some had been knocked down.

"We'll guide on those towers," he said. "And it's a good thing we've got something to guide on, because this is going to be a night attack. The Japanese have been attacking at night all through the war. Well, we're going to give them a taste of their own medicine. We're going to pull out at 2:30 in the morning and hit that position before dawn."

As usual, the weather was cloudy with intermittent showers. There would be no moon that night. To enable each man to follow the one in front of him, Desmond handed out small gauze patches to be placed on the back of each man's pack. He hoped that the white spots could be seen in the dark.

Lieutenant Gornto had come down with pneumonia during the battle for the escarpment. A young officer replaced him. When the men started out through such utter darkness that they could not even see the white patch on the man in front of them, they had the chill feeling that this mission could not possibly end in anything but disaster. But such was the leadership of Captain Vernon that even the new men, who had known him for but a few days, followed with only a nominal amount of complaining.

They moved on through the torn-up terrain in a column of threes. The white squares might have been pitch black. They weren't visible. After several men had gotten lost, word was passed back for each man to hang on to the one in front of him. Occasionally flares went up, illuminating the valley in a harsh white light. Every man fell face down on his hands so that no white would show.

There was to be no sound. Rifles were emptied, bayonets attached. One Japanese soldier was encountered. Vernon gave one of his officers permission to put one shell in his carbine and use it.

Before long they had lost the path of the shot-up power structures. Frequent stops had to be made for the officers to check their compasses and to enable the men to catch up and get organized. But even then, as they neared the objective, the platoons became separated. No one will ever know for sure, but some of the men have always suspected that it was one platoon firing on another, rather than the Japanese, that gave their position away. No longer could they hope to make a surprise attack. The Japanese began throwing grenades. Two men were killed immediately. The rest sought cover.

More by feel than by sight, Desmond knew that the company had passed over the brow of a small hill and was proceeding down the back side when the shooting started. He and two riflemen stumbled into a shell hole and stayed there. One of the men grabbed Desmond by the arm. "Look!" came a hoarse whisper.

A Japanese soldier was silhouetted dimly against the skyline. He moved, and Desmond saw the sputtering fuse of a hand grenade coming straight to the shell hole. It landed right at his feet. The two other men were on the other side of the hole.

Instantaneously, by reflex action, like a farm boy getting close to a kicking mule, Desmond put his foot on the grenade. A split second later it exploded. He felt a jolt. It didn't hurt. Rather, it numbed him. He felt as though he was flying through the air head over heels. It knocked all the wind out of him. He shook his head and opened his eyes. He was still alive. The two men in the hole with him had gone, but the Japanese soldier was still there. Another grenade came sputtering through the night, but missed. Without thinking of how badly he was hurt, Desmond crawled out of that hole. Making his way through the underbrush, he called softly, over and over, "It's Doss, I'm hit." No one answered. He kept crawling until he was out of range of the grenades.

From far away he heard someone say that the company was withdrawing. He started crawling up the hill, dragging his left leg after him. It was throbbing all the way down from hip to toe. He ran his hand along his thigh, down the calf. It was wet with blood all the way down. He realized that he had lost, and was still losing, a lot of blood, but he could not stop in the midst of the retreat to attend to himself. He felt himself passing out. *What do you do for shock and loss of blood? You elevate the patient's feet.* Dutifully Desmond squirmed around so that he was lying with his head pointing downhill. He remained in that position until he felt the consciousness returning with the blood running into his brain. He began doggedly crawling up the hill again until he started blacking out, then turned around to lie with his head downhill.

Finally he reached the top of the hill and started down the other side. The first light of dawn was beginning to appear. He came to a shell hole.

"Who's there?" a voice whispered.

"Me, Doss."

"You're just the man I want to see," the soldier said. "I've been hit in the shoulder."

Working in the dim light, Desmond dressed the man's wounds. Then he checked himself. Reaching down into his trouser leg, he felt dried clots of blood, like pebbles. He pulled out a handful. But he couldn't work through his bloody trouser leg and he pulled his pants off. He felt down his left leg. Blood was running out of holes from his buttocks on down to his ankle. He could feel pieces of metal embedded in his flesh. He bandaged himself as best he could.

He knew he could crawl no farther, and resigned himself to staying in the hole until daybreak. At least he had company. The hole was shallow, and he borrowed the soldier's shovel and tried to dig it out more. It was hard going and he gave up. He blacked out with his feet sticking out of the hole. When he opened his eyes it was light. He looked around him. The first thing he saw was a large artillery shell, unexploded, just inches from his head. He had been digging around it with the shovel. If he had hit it . . . The thought of that knocked him into full consciousness.

The man with the shoulder wound had also lapsed into a coma, but Doss managed to rouse him. They decided to stay where they were and hope litter bearers would find them. Now Doss's wound was extremely painful. He took out a morphine syrette and showed the other soldier how to inject it. But the rifleman, squeamish about sticking the needle in the skin, squirted most of the morphine on his sleeve. Desmond finally gave himself the shot.

The company was beginning to pull itself together again. Desmond heard someone shout that Captain Vernon had been hit. He shouted back and started dragging himself in that direction. But Vernon came to him. Blood flowed out of the captain's mouth and dripped off his chin. A fragment of a hand grenade had passed through his mouth and out through his cheek.

"You have to go back, captain," Doss told him.

Captain Vernon gave a short little laugh. "I'm staying up here with my men, Doss," he mumbled through his torn mouth. Desmond knew it was useless to argue with him. He patched up the wound as best he could.

"Our artillery is going to drop a barrage on this area this morning," Vernon said. "We got to get word back to hold it."

But they had no communications. The company's radio was shot. Messengers were sent out. One located another unit with a functioning set, and they sent word to headquarters to call off the artillery.

In the meantime, of course, no litter bearers came into the area. Finally they arrived. One of them, T/5 Ralph E. Baker, knew Doss well. He immediately took over and quickly had his friend and fellow medic on the way back to the battalion aid station.

They had a long way to hike through a dangerous area on a day that had turned hot and muggy. Desmond drifted in and out of consciousness. He woke up with a jolt. Shells cracked through the trees. Enemy tanks fired in their direction. The four litter bearers had dropped to the ground, and Desmond had hit the dirt with them. The pain was agonizing, and it brought him completely to his senses. He looked around. Not ten feet away lay another wounded American soldier. Blood was all over his head, but he was breathing. Desmond instantly knew that this man's wound was more serious than his own.

When the shooting subsided and the four litter bearers got ready to proceed, Desmond rolled off the litter. "This man's hit in the head," he said. "You'd better take him."

Baker and the other three men protested vigorously. Desmond was their friend. "You're the one we started out with, Doss," Baker said. "We want to get you back safely."

"No, sir," Doss insisted. "You know that a head wound takes precedence. You get this man back. I can last a long time yet. Nobody knows how long this guy can last."

He finally convinced them. They rolled the unconscious man on the litter and left Desmond there alone. But before long someone else came along the trail. Doss recognized him immediately. He was Lewis Brooks from Richmond. He had been hit, but he could walk, and he offered to help Doss as best he could. Doss climbed to his feet and put his left arm around Brooks's neck. Brooks supported him with an arm around his waist. They started hobbling over the beat-up terrain toward the aid station.

Something hit Desmond's arm, the one around Brooks's neck, like a blow from a hammer. Instantly after he heard a rifle shot. Sniper! The bullet passed through Desmond's forearm and lodged in his upper arm. He knew it had broken the bones both above and below the elbow. But if it hadn't been for his arm it would have hit Brooks in the chest or throat. The two men hit the ground. They spotted a shell hole and wormed their way to it. Desmond had to hold on to his arm to keep it from flapping loosely. Crawling with one leg and two arms out of commission was not easy.

"What can we do?" Brooks wanted to know. "There aren't any medics to help you."

"You're all the medic I need."

"Who, me?" Brooks asked. "What can I do?"

"I'll show you. Give me the stock off your rifle."

Brooks took his rifle down and threw the barrel away. Desmond had left his aid kits back on a hill, but he still had his field jacket with him. He handed it to Brooks. "Here, wrap the stock in this. Now see if you can tear some strips off my shirt and tie my arm to it. Then tie the whole thing against my side."

Lying in the shell hole, Brooks managed to do it. Then they started out again. They could only hope that the sniper had moved on. Both of Desmond's wounds were now excruciatingly painful. The pieces of metal in his leg and buttocks—seventeen in all—cut his flesh and scraped against the bone whenever he moved his leg. He suffered from shock and loss of blood.

"I can't walk any farther," he suddenly told Brooks.

"Do you want to sit down?" Brooks asked.

Desmond thought about that a moment. Sit on what? That ripped and torn buttock? "No," he said.

"How about lying down, then?" Brooks asked.

Desmond could only shake his head. Things got blacker and blacker. He felt himself slowly crumpling to the ground.

CHAPTER 6

THE GREATEST HONOR

Corporal," the voice behind him called. "Corporal Doss."

Desmond started, and pulled himself out of his reverie. Outside the hospital window the countryside of his beloved Virginia was beginning to turn red and brown and yellow with the colors of fall.

Desmond turned around, and began trying to stand at attention. Standing there was Colonel Hackett L. Connor, commanding officer of the hospital. He had a most uncolonel-like grin on his face.

"As you were, corporal!" he said, putting Desmond at ease. "Your promotion just came through and I thought I'd tell you about it myself."

"Thank you, sir," Desmond answered. In spite of the colonel's friendly tone, Desmond could not relax completely. He still found it hard to believe he was really here, home, safe, alive, near his loved ones, the war over. For months he had been living in a world of half blissful dream, half horrid nightmare. The war had gone on so long, so terribly long ...

He had awakened at the battalion aid station. They'd given him a massive shot of morphine, and he went back into a fog. Then he found himself in a field hospital far behind the lines, sitting on an operating table. The pain was excruciating both where he sat and where the doctors manipulated his broken arm.

"I can't sit down," he muttered. "It hurts."

"You have to. It's the only way we can get this cast on," one of the doctors insisted.

"I don't want to sit down," Doss murmured. He felt himself slipping into unconsciousness again. Suddenly a piercing odor went up his nose and his head cleared. Someone had broken an ammonia capsule under his nose.

"You've got to stay awake," someone ordered.

Keeping him conscious with ammonia and conversation, the doctors and their assistants put a plaster cast on the entire upper part of his body. The cast held his arm out parallel with the ground, but bent at the elbow. When the plaster hardened, they finally let him get off his torn rear end. Then they could give him ether, and they put him under before they started extricating the jagged pieces of metal imbedded in his leg.

Later, in an ambulance, he bumped over an Okinawan road to the harbor where a hospital ship waited. A big, clumsy cast covered him from the waist to the neck. Bandages coiled around his ripped leg. What part of him was left was stark naked, under the GI blanket.

His Bible! *Where was Dorothy's Bible?* He felt for it with his good hand. It wasn't there.

At the dock he called the ambulance driver. "My Bible," he gasped. "I've lost my Bible!"

"Sure," soothed the driver. "They'll get you one on the ship."

"No, no!" Desmond cried, almost in hysterics. "I want *my* Bible, the one my wife gave me." He insisted that the driver pass the word to his friends at the battalion aid station, asking them to look for his Bible, his Bible with Dorothy's letter in it. In his agitation he didn't realize what a forlorn hope that was. You don't call off wars to search the jungle for a Bible!

Gradually he came around. His leg began to heal, although it would be some time before he could walk on it. The plaster cast was miserably uncomfortable, but Desmond knew he could live with it because he was going home.

The hospital ship took him to Guam. From there he was flown to Hawaii, where he remained for several impatient weeks. Inside the cast he felt filthy; he couldn't stand his own smell. He saw another patient in a light cast made of aluminum tubing.

"Why can't I have one of those?" he asked one of the ward attendants.

"Because yours is in fairly good shape," the attendant explained, and looked at his fellow medic meaningfully.

Desmond got it. He began working on his cast, soaking it, picking at it, and it didn't take him long to wreck it. He got his new, light, airplane splint.

Finally, two months after he'd been hit, he reached the United States. From Fort Lewis, Washington, he called Dorothy and heard her voice again for the first time in two years.

Each leg of the long journey home took an agonizingly long time. It was military policy to send each man as close to home as possible. Desmond wound up at the Army hospital at Swannanoa, North Carolina. His mother and father came to see him there.

Dorothy, however, had gone back to college and was within days of getting her degree. Desmond was promised a furlough as soon as he could get around, and he insisted that Dorothy stay on and graduate. By that time he could come to her.

Finally that day came. His arm stuck out clumsily in the crowded bus, and the granulated tissue in his leg wounds was painful, especially where he sat down.

But he was going home.

Desmond had fought through three major campaigns, maintaining his composure and determination while others about him cracked from the strain. In a crowded bus station more than ten thousand miles from the fighting front, in the arms of his loved one, Desmond finally permitted the tears to course unashamedly down his cheeks. They were tears of joy.

In the midst of this happiness he did not forget to thank the Lord above for deliverance from death. Out of his monthly pay he took a second tithe for his church, in gratitude for being permitted to return alive.

While at Swannanoa he received a warm and welcome letter from his friend Sergeant Howell in the medical battalion. All Desmond's old buddies sent their best. The division newspaper had published an exciting account of his heroism on the escarpment; Howell enclosed it. There was talk that Desmond was being recommended for a high decoration, perhaps even the Congressional Medal of Honor. One news item shocked and saddened him: Captain Vernon had been killed when a mortar shell scored a direct hit on the company command post.

And they had found Desmond's Bible! The whole company had turned out to look for it. Desmond saw, in his imagination, the green-clad soldiers fanning out, poking in shell holes, under debris, all the time keeping a sharp lookout for booby traps and snipers. He couldn't hold back the tears. To think that those men would do that for him! It could only mean that they felt for him the love and respect he felt for them.

Not only was the Bible hunt a great compliment and tribute to him, but he also gloried in the realization that this search for the Holy Bible surely brought those men closer to God.

The Bible was sent to Dorothy. Though waterlogged, with the cover falling off, it was still in reasonable condition, and later Desmond had it rebound. Tucked in its place was the lesson he had been working on, dated May 26, 1945. He had been wounded on May 21, a Monday.

When finally the bones had knit sufficiently so that the cast could be removed, the next stop was the Woodrow Wilson Hospital near Staunton, Virginia. Here he underwent an operation for removal of the bullet from his arm. At last the future seemed positive. It was early October 1945. The war was over, both in Europe and in Japan. The boys were coming home.

And here he was, *Corporal* Doss. "And that isn't all, corporal," Colonel Conner was saying. "I have a very great honor. I can inform you that you have been awarded the Congressional Medal of Honor, our country's highest honor."

"Sir?" Desmond asked. "Er, I mean—" His voice trailed off. The Congressional Medal of Honor, the nation's highest decoration, presented only to the nation's heroes for outstanding gallantry beyond the call of duty in actual combat. No sailor, no soldier, no marine, no general, no admiral could receive a greater award.

Through his mind raced a jumble of conflicting emotions. Gratitude, pride, vindication. He remembered that miserable night in the barracks at Fort Jackson when the Army shoes had come hurtling over the beds toward a scared young inductee on his knees in prayer. Now those men and others like them, officers and men he had served with in training and in battle, had recommended him for the nation's highest award.

There was sadness too, and grief. Desmond thought of Clarence Glenn, with the cheerful face that could smile no more; Herb Schechter, whose quiet, sincere voice would never be heard again; intrepid Captain Vernon, who had given his last order; all the other good buddies who had paid the supreme price.

Even at such a moment, Desmond Doss thought of others. They, he thought, were the ones who deserved that honor. And in keeping with his religious convictions, he thought too of the Power which had brought him through safely. He bowed his head and gave humble thanks to God.

The presentation of the medal was to be made at the White House, several days hence. A few days after Colonel Conner first told Desmond, he met him in the hall again. Desmond still had his Pfc stripe on.

"If I ever see that stripe on you again I'll rip it off myself," the colonel said. He sent a member of his staff, a lieutenant, to see to it that Desmond was outfitted with a complete new uniform and all the proper regalia. In addition to the corporal stripes on each arm, on his left arm he wore the Statue of Liberty patch of the 77th Division, two small gold horizontal stripes representing two six-month periods overseas, and a diagonal hash mark representing three years in the service. Over his left breast pocket he wore ribbons signifying the Bronze Star for valor, with cluster, the Purple Heart with two Oak Leaves, the Good Conduct Medal, the American ribbon with three bronze stars for the Asiatic-Pacific Campaign (Okinawa, Guam, and Leyte, with arrowhead for amphibious landing), and the Philippine Liberation with one star. Over this Christmas tree was the combat medic badge. Over his right shirt pocket he wore the small blue ribbon representing the Presidential unit citation given the 1st Battalion, 307th Infantry "for assaulting, capturing and securing the Escarpment."

Three days before the ceremony a member of the hospital staff brought Dorothy from Richmond to the hospital. The colonel furnished his official command car, with driver, for the 150-mile trip to Washington. Desmond was one of fifteen men to be awarded the medal in one ceremony on the White House lawn. For three days before that, however, they had the run of the town. Desmond and Dorothy, and Desmond's parents, stayed at the Willard Hotel, guests of the United States of America. They had a luxurious suite.

Then came the presentation ceremony. Desmond looked around at the other men gathered on the White House lawn. Thanks to his ideas of entertainment, he was unquestionably the freshest one there. One man showed up late with an obvious hangover.

Standing rigidly at attention, waiting to approach Harry S. Truman, the President of the United States, and receive a medal, then to receive the congratulations of General of the Army George Catlett Marshall, Desmond felt his knees shaking. One man after another stepped forward, heard his individual citation read by the President's aide, then as newsreel cameramen and newspaper photographers took his picture, received the medal and a handshake from the President. Desmond expected to be nervous, ill at ease, and embarrassed when he met President Truman.

His turn came. He walked forward and stopped, as rehearsed, at a line laid in the grass in front of the President. Truman obviously knew Doss's identity. He did something he had not done with the others. He stepped across the line, gave Desmond a hearty handshake, and made him feel at ease. The President held on to Desmond's hand all the time the citation was being read.

This is what Desmond heard:

Private First Class Desmond T. Doss was a company aid man with the 307th Infantry Medical Detachment when the 1st Battalion of that regiment assaulted a jagged escarpment 400 feet high near Orasoo-Mura, Okinawa, Ryukyu Islands, on April 29, 1945.

As our troops gained the summit, a heavy concentration of artillery, mortar, and machine-gun fire crashed into them, inflicting approximately seventy-five casualties and driving the others back. Private Doss refused to seek cover and remained in the fire-swept area with the many stricken, carrying them one by one to the edge of the escarpment and there lowering them on a rope-supported litter down the face of a cliff to friendly hands.

On May 2, he exposed himself to heavy rifle and mortar fire in rescuing a wounded man 200 yards forward of the lines on the same escarpment; and two days later he treated four men who had been cut down while assaulting a strongly defended cave, advancing through a shower of grenades to within eight yards of enemy forces in a cave's mouth, where he dressed his comrades' wounds before making four separate trips under fire to evacuate them to safety.

On May 5, he unhesitatingly braved enemy shelling and small-arms fire to assist an artillery officer. He applied bandages, moved his patient to a spot that offered protection from small-arms fire, and, while artillery and mortar shells fell close by, painstakingly administered plasma. Later that day, when an American was severely wounded by fire from a cave, Private Doss crawled to him where he had fallen twenty-five feet from the enemy position, rendered aid, and carried him 100 yards to safety while continually exposed to enemy fire.

On May 21, in a night attack on high ground near Shuri, he remained in exposed territory while the rest of his company took cover, fearlessly risking the chance that he would be mistaken for an infiltrating Japanese and giving aid to the injured until he was himself seriously wounded in the legs by the explosion of a grenade. Rather than call another aid man from cover, he cared for his own injuries and waited five hours before litter bearers reached him and started carrying him to cover.

The trio was caught in an enemy tank attack and Private Doss, seeing a more critically wounded man nearby, crawled off the litter and directed the bearers to give their first attention to the other man. Awaiting the litter bearers' return, he was again struck, this time suffering a compound fracture of one arm. With magnificent fortitude he bound a rifle stock to his shattered arm as a splint and then crawled 300 yards over rough terrain to the aid station.

Through his outstanding bravery and unflinching determination in the face of desperately dangerous conditions Private Doss saved the lives of many soldiers. His name became a symbol throughout the 77th Infantry Division for outstanding gallantry far above and beyond the call of duty. [4]

"I'm proud of you," the President said. "You really deserve this. I consider this a greater honor than being President." Then he hung the medal, the nation's highest honor, around Desmond's neck.

After that, General Marshall came down the line and congratulated the medal winners. This was another thrill. Desmond had carried that document signed by Marshall, stipulating he would not be forced to bear arms, all during the war.

The War Department had put out a full press release on Desmond's being awarded the medal. His escort obtained several copies of it, and Desmond and Dorothy and their parents read it together:

---

4   Though the events described in the citation are of course true, they were based on the hasty recollections of men immediately following the actions described, and their sequence is not in exact order.

A conscientious objector who was assigned to the Medical Corps, United States Army, Private First Class Desmond T. Doss, of Lynchburg, Virginia, displayed such outstanding bravery and unflinching determination in aiding his wounded comrades in the fierce Okinawa campaign that he has been awarded the Medal of Honor, it was announced today by the War Department.

The Nation's highest decoration goes to the twenty-six-year-old soldier who, although not bearing arms, performed so many feats of heroism on the battlefields of Guam, Leyte, and Okinawa that his name became a symbol for outstanding gallantry throughout the 77th Infantry "Statue of Liberty" Division.

Private Doss's wife, Dorothy Pauline, lives at Route 9, Box 66, Richmond, Virginia; and his parents, Mr. and Mrs. William T. Doss, reside at 1835 Easley Avenue, Lynchburg.

The medal will be presented to Private Doss by President Truman at the White House on Friday, October 12.

Private Doss, a member of the 307th Infantry Medical Detachment, 1st Battalion, received the unstinting praise of fighting men of the 77th Division from generals to privates.

Brigadier General Edwin H. Randle, commanding general of the division, asserted, "This soldier by his unfailing devotion to duty and his gallantry and intrepidity at the risk of his life above and beyond the call of duty has gained the respect, admiration, and affection of the entire division."

This is the more noteworthy as, on being inducted into the military service, Private Doss was, and still is, a conscientious objector. He refused to carry arms or even touch a weapon. His organization commander transferred him to the battalion medical detachment where he was made company aid man because he wanted to be forward with the men.

In the Guam and Leyte campaigns Private Doss demonstrated the same qualities. No matter how heavy the fire, he remained and cared for wounded men regardless of consequences or danger.

Private Doss was awarded the Medal of Honor for specific acts of supreme heroism on Okinawa in the Ryukyu Islands between April 29 and May 21, 1945.

First Lieutenant Onless C. Brister, 245 Central Avenue, Winona, Mississippi, pointed out, "Private Doss was at all times up with the front lines to care for injured men. In several instances he braved intense enemy small-arms and mortar fire to give aid and to move men who were wounded."

First Lieutenant Cecil L. Gornto, of Live Oak, Florida, was 1st Platoon leader of Company B to which Private Doss was attached from April 29 to May 8.

"On the morning of April 29," Lieutenant Gornto related, "heavy mortar fire was falling in the area, and someone called for a medic. Private Doss left his hole and climbed to the top of the hill. He found the wounded man in total darkness and gave him first aid. As soon as it was light enough, I observed him lowering the wounded man over the cliff on a rope to evacuate him. This man had both legs blown off."

Another link in the Doss chain of sterling heroism was told by Second Lieutenant Kenneth L. Phillips, Route 3, Lexington, North Carolina.

"On May 5, during an intense grenade battle in the vicinity of Kakazu," Lieutenant Phillips said, "four men were badly wounded while trying to blow up a cave. They were lying under a vicious hail of grenade and mortar fire. With total disregard for his own personal safety, Private Doss went forth four times and pulled the wounded men to safety."

Private First Class Carl B. Bentley, of Fulshear, Texas, spoke of an instance on May 2.

"Private Doss was told of a man out in the front lines between our line and the Japs. He went out and brought this man in under very heavy rifle and knee-mortar fire."

The climax in the Virginian's amazing battle career as a male angel of mercy occurred on the night of May 21, when he was badly injured, thereby winning an Oak Leaf Cluster to the Purple Heart he earned May 10, when he was less seriously wounded. Technician Fifth Grade Ralph E. Baker, of the 1st Battalion medics, tells the story.

"On May 21, Private Doss was wounded by an enemy grenade. Instead of calling another aid man from the safety of his foxhole, Private Doss treated his own wounds and gave himself a shot of morphine when the pain became too great.

"Litter bearers reached him in the morning, almost six hours later. After they carried him about fifty yards, the litter bearers were halted momentarily by bursts of mortar fire. Private Doss crawled off the litter and told the aid men to take more seriously wounded men in first.

"He was wounded a second time while he lay there. He bound a rifle stock to his shattered arm to form a splint and crawled to the aid station despite his wounds."

Private Doss, who was born February 7, 1919, in Lynchburg, entered the Army at Camp Lee, Virginia, on April 1, 1942. He was a ship joiner before his induction. He was awarded the Bronze Star for his meritorious service as a medical aid man on Leyte in the Philippine Islands from December 7 to 21, 1944. [5]

To top it all, Desmond was given a ten-day furlough. He and Dorothy went to her home in Richmond. For weeks he had been trying to get transferred to the McGuire General Hospital there. He was now able to get around fairly well. His leg was almost as good as new, except for a few small fragments of metal which remained in it and occasionally caused pain. The bones in his shattered arm had knit, the bullet had been removed, and the incision was healing well. Desmond had been told that he would not be able to use the arm again, but he believed that with God's help and his own continued effort and exercise he would develop strength and mobility in it.

In the near future he would receive his honorable discharge. He had not yet decided whether he would arrange to be discharged out of the special provisions granted a winner of the Congressional Medal of Honor, as a disabled veteran, or on the basis of the large number of discharge points he had earned overseas and in combat.

Pending his separation from the service, it would be a great convenience if he could be stationed at McGuire, to be near Dorothy. One day he dropped in to the hospital to ask if he could in any way expedite the transfer from Woodrow Wilson. Papers throughout the country, indeed all over the world, had carried the story of the conscientious objector who had won the Congressional Medal of Honor. In Richmond, because of Dorothy's connection with the city, the papers had devoted large spreads to the

---

5   Again there are small discrepancies.

hero-medic. When he entered the administration building, he was recognized immediately and escorted into the office of the commanding officer.

"You don't need to have a transfer," Desmond was told. "You don't even have to go back to Woodrow Wilson. We'll send word back there you weren't feeling well and checked in with us while you were here on furlough."

"Oh, no," Desmond said, unused to cutting corners in the military, "I'll go back there and check out personally."

In the meantime Desmond had to make another appearance. His hometown, Lynchburg, was clamoring for him to come back for a hero's welcome. Plans were quickly made. He was met at the station by city officials and driven down Main Street in an open car in a full military parade. Bands played and banners proclaimed him the "Wonder Man of Okinawa." Post 16 of the American Legion gave him a life membership.

Late in October, Desmond returned to Woodrow Wilson to make his transfer. Colonel Conner met him with a big salute. When Desmond looked embarrassed the colonel said, "Remember, soldier, the Medal of Honor rates the salute of a five-star general." [6]

And so Desmond returned to McGuire, in Richmond. He had a Class A pass, which meant that he could come and go as he liked. He had long been thinking about what he would like to do when he got out of the service. Though some strength was beginning to come back to his left arm, he knew he would not be able to go back to his old trade of carpentry, or, indeed, any craft which required two good arms. He was exploring, however, two interesting avenues of financial fulfillment.

While at Swannanoa Hospital he had spent a weekend at the home of a friend who was a florist. The friend had had to make a few wreaths, and Desmond had helped. He was pleased with the wreath he had made; he thought it as good as that made by the professionals.

Desmond had always loved flowers. As a child, then as a youth, he had cultivated flowers and flowering shrubs. Now there was much talk of the

---

6   This is a common misconception. Many high officers salute Medal of Honor winners, but it is a matter of individual choice, not a requirement. Regulations did, in 1945, provide that a Medal of Honor man may travel in a military aircraft when space is available, that his son may get special assistance with an appointment to West Point or Annapolis, that he would receive $2 per month and a pension of $120 a year at the age of 65.

GI Bill of Rights which would help veterans in their adjustment to peace. Perhaps, Desmond thought, the new legislation would in some way make it possible for him to learn more about flowers and the florist business, and perhaps even have his own florist shop.

The other avenue was also concerned with living, beautiful organisms, though somewhat different from flowers. In Richmond one day he passed a small shop featuring tropical fish, and he became interested in them. The proprietor appreciated his interest and whetted it. A man could earn a comfortable and pleasant living raising and selling exotic fish, he said.

Surely now Desmond would, in the words of the ninety-first psalm, "abide under the shadow of the Almighty." His Army pay and allotment continued. He wore the nation's highest decoration.

At long last he and Dorothy could begin to raise that family of which they had dreamed so many years. They both loved children. They were young and brave and positive that they could provide for those children in a Christian home.

If it were possible to make Desmond's faith in God any stronger, to increase his desire to serve the Lord and his fellowman and to spread the gospel, then his ordeal in the South Pacific had done just that. Too many times he had crossed areas exposed to small-arms, mortar, even artillery fire on an errand of mercy without being scratched, not to believe that the Lord was protecting him. He had been wounded, yes, and seriously so, but he was alive, and home, and healthy—and he was thankful.

He further resolved that, as a tribute and in gratitude to the glory of God, he would go anywhere the church asked him, speak to whatever group wanted to hear him, and in any and every way advance the work of the Lord and the church.

THE FAITH THAT
SHAPED THE MAN

INTRODUCTION TO THE MAN

Do you know who that is?" The deacon elbowed my ribs, his eyes wide with excitement. He was pointing to an older gentleman making his way to the front of our small country church. I didn't recognize the man at first, but I didn't have to wait long to find out. "*That's* Desmond Doss!"

And right away, I couldn't help but feel the same excitement. I had just read Desmond's amazing story, *The Unlikeliest Hero*, to my kids—and like me, they were moved by the thrilling tales of his steady faith and sacrificial courage as an American soldier during World War II.

That was the day I first met Desmond and his wife. Her family happened to be members of the church I was pastoring in Northern California, so the two would visit our congregation from time to time. As we spoke together that day, the signs of Desmond's time in combat were hard to miss. For instance, the deafening sounds of battle, along with some experimental antibiotics, had severely damaged his hearing, so he wore a cochlear implant. The device was powered by a small battery receiver that hung around his neck, much like a battle badge of honor.

Of course, Desmond went on to receive the highest military honor in the land, hung around his neck by then U.S. President Harry Truman. Indeed, he was the first conscientious objector to receive the distinguished Medal of Honor, awarded to him for personal acts of valor above and beyond the call of duty. But what struck me the most about Desmond was his quiet, humble manner despite these honors—whenever someone asked him about his incredible experiences during World War II, he always smiled and gave God the credit.

Subsequently, we met and spoke together many times over the years, and it's not surprising to me or anyone else who knew Desmond that he would be the subject of numerous books and films, including the 2004 documentary *The Conscientious Objector* and the most recent Hollywood film *Hacksaw Ridge*.

Yet while Doss' service in the military and his heroic sacrifice on the battlefield are now well known, few have delved deeply into the unique beliefs that helped shape this Christian hero. Desmond was a Seventh-day Adventist, a denomination that has received growing attention due in part to the release of Mel Gibson's movie about him, and to prominent Adventists such as Ben Carson, who ran for president of the United States.

But who are the Seventh-day Adventists? What do they believe about the Bible—and why? They comprise one of the fastest-growing denominations in the world, so it's worth exploring the truth about this group of religious people and what drives them.

Doug Batchelor
President, Amazing Facts

THE BIBLE FIRST

War or no war, Desmond Doss was a firm believer in reading his Bible. The pocket edition, given to him by his wife before he left for Guam, was so precious to him that he carried it with him everywhere. When he was eventually wounded and taken by ambulance to an army hospital ship, he discovered that he had lost his most valued possession. Word was passed to his friends who went back to the battlefield and eventually found the Bible and sent it to him.

If you have never heard of Seventh-day Adventists, or if you are unfamiliar with their beliefs, their simplest description is that they are strong believers in the Bible. Like Desmond, Adventists proclaim a love for the Scriptures and believe their unique doctrines stand on the Word of God. As you have read this amazing story of Desmond Doss, I am sure that many of you have questions about Desmond's religion that he believed in so strongly. But who and what are the Seventh-day Adventists and what are their beliefs? In these next few pages, we'll explore the common beliefs Adventists share with mainstream Christianity—and those beliefs that are unique to them.

Bible Christians

Not everyone who calls himself a Baptist, Methodist, Catholic, or member of another denomination, faithfully exemplifies those denominations—or even knows clearly what they teach. All churches can have truth and errors spoken about them by people or websites out to misrepresent their teachings.

So if you want to know what a denomination believes, you need to look at its basic teachings. The very first Seventh-day Adventist core belief states:

"The Holy Scriptures, Old and New Testaments, are the written Word of God, given by divine inspiration. The inspired authors spoke and wrote as they were moved by the Holy Spirit. In this Word, God has committed to humanity the knowledge necessary for salvation. The Holy Scriptures are the supreme, authoritative, and the infallible revelation of His will. They are the standard of character, the test of experience, the definitive revealer of doctrines, and the trustworthy record of God's acts in history." [7]

Adventists, like most mainline Christians, believe that Jesus personally upheld the importance of the Word of God. He said, "Heaven and earth will pass away, but My words will by no means pass away" (Matthew 24:35). He also stated, "Man shall not live by bread alone, but by every word that proceeds from the mouth of God" (Matthew 4:4). This foundational belief sets the framework for all their other teachings. Seventh-day Adventists believe that everything a church, pastor, teacher, or prophet says must be measured against God's Word, the Bible. This is why Desmond only needed one book—the Bible—to keep him going throughout his horrific experience in World War II.

Discovering God

Sometimes Hollywood takes liberties in dramatizing true-life stories in order to draw crowds, but in so doing the real person gets lost behind romanticized footage. The same thing has happened with God. So many false ideas of God's character have been presented that people find it difficult to understand what the Creator really desires.

Seventh-day Adventists believe the only source of truth about God is the Bible and that within its pages one will discover that heaven sent a gift to our world to remove all doubt about the nature of God—the gift of Jesus Christ. The central focus of the Scriptures is a revelation of a loving God who is made known through Jesus, the Son of God. Adventists believe:

"God the eternal Son became incarnate in Jesus Christ. Through Him all things were created, the character of God is revealed, the salvation of humanity is accomplished, and the world is judged. Forever truly God, He became also truly human, Jesus the Christ." [8]

---

7   You can find a complete list of the twenty-eight Seventh-day Adventist core beliefs at https://www.adventist.org/en/beliefs

8   https://www.adventist.org/en/beliefs/god/son/

Seventh-day Adventists also believe in the Trinity. Though that word itself is not found in the Bible, Adventists believe that God the Father, God the Son, and God the Spirit comprise the totality of the infinite God. As such, Adventists do not believe Jesus was a created being. Adventists believe the Bible teaches that Jesus has always existed (John 1:1–3) and through Christ all things were made (see Hebrews 1:1–2).

They also do not believe the Holy Spirit is merely a dynamic, impersonal force that floats around and is used by God. The Bible teaches that the Holy Spirit is a person. Jesus said, "When He, the Spirit of truth, has come, He will guide you into all truth" (John 16:13). The Holy Spirit is considered equal with God the Father and God the Son, since Jesus included the Spirit in His instructions on baptizing people: "In the name of the Father and of the Son and of the Holy Spirit" (Matthew 28:19).

Creation

Closely connected to the Adventist understanding of God is the story of human beginnings. Seventh-day Adventists believe that God is the Creator of all things and has shown in the Bible an accurate account of His work in making our world. In accordance with the Scriptures, "In six days the LORD made the heavens and the earth, the sea, and all that is in them" (Exodus 20:11).

It was through Jesus, God the Son, that the earth was formed. "God, who at various times and in various ways spoke in time past to the fathers by the prophets, has in these last days spoken to us by His Son, whom He has appointed heir of all things, through whom also He made the worlds" (Hebrews 1:1, 2).

Evidences in science and geology continue to affirm the hand of a divine Designer. Growing numbers of scientists[9] believe that our earth was not a cosmic accident that evolved over billions of years. Rather, "By faith we understand that the worlds were framed by the word of God, so that the things which are seen were not made of things which are visible" (Hebrews 11:3). Thus, Adventists have concluded that God the Son was not dependent on pre-existing matter to form the universe.

Some brush off the Creation story as unimportant, but Adventists believe a deeper look at the first two chapters of Genesis in the Bible reveal

---

9   See http://creation.com/creation-scientists and http://www.christiananswers.net/q-eden/edn-scientists.html

many of the key teachings and values found throughout the rest of the Bible. For instance, Creation reminds us that God is the maker of all things and we are His children. Because the Lord is the creator, He alone is worthy of worship.

Creation also shows us that on the seventh day God ended His work and blessed that day as sacred. Sabbath is a memorial of Creation and as people worship each week they are reminded that our world was made by a loving God, and not by some theoretical Big Bang that took place eons ago.

A Brief History of the Movement

In the early part of the nineteenth century, a great revival gripped a vast swath in the United States and parts of Europe—it was called the Second Great Awakening. It began around 1790 but grew rapidly after 1820, especially among Baptist and Methodist congregations. Within this revival was a movement uniquely focused on the soon coming of Jesus in the 1830s and 1840s, a movement sparked by the preaching of a sincere Baptist evangelist named William Miller.

Miller concluded, after an in-depth, years-long study of the book of Daniel, that Jesus would come in October of 1844. When that date passed and Christ didn't come, many people lost interest in the prophecies of Daniel and Revelation. This "great disappointment," as it was called, was a turning point. Some members from different denominations believed they misunderstood the prophecies and so they gathered to study them more deeply. Setting aside their other doctrinal differences, they prayerfully opened the Word of God and searched the Scriptures.

As they studied with open hearts, this small group of believers was surprised to discover that church teachings were based on human tradition, not on the Bible. They met in a series of "Bible conferences" over the next fifteen years and identified many Bible truths forgotten since the time of the early Christian church. From their earnest study grew the Seventh-day Adventist Church, a movement which now has nearly nineteen million members. [10]

Today, Seventh-day Adventists worship in over 80,000 churches around the world. Their work is progressing in 215 of the 237 countries and areas of the world recognized by the United Nations. Adventists publish and

---

10   Membership as of 2014: 18,479,257 (https://www.adventist.org/en/information/statistics/article/go/-/seventh-day-adventist-world-church-statistics-2014/)

preach in 974 languages and provide education to 1.8 million children and youth in over 7,700 schools and training institutions. Fifteen media centers and sixty-two publishing houses help spread their message everywhere.

The Name "Seventh-day Adventist"

With over 40,000 Christian denominations[11] and many with similar sounding names, it can be confusing to sort out what different churches believe. So, why would a church choose the name Seventh-day Adventist?

The term "Seventh-day" speaks of the Adventist belief that God wants us to keep all of His Ten Commandments, including the fourth, which says, "Remember the Sabbath day, to keep it holy" (Exodus 20:8). That is why Seventh-day Adventists worship on Saturday, the seventh day of the week. They see no evidence in the Bible or history that God has changed this day to Sunday or to any other day of the week.

The Sabbath is a special time each week that Adventists meet to worship God, fellowship with others, and enjoy God's creation. It is a day of rest as well as a reminder that God saves and sanctifies people (Ezekiel 20:12). Seventh-day Adventists keep the Sabbath, not to earn salvation, but as a response of love to the Creator who desires to meet with His people.

The word "Adventist" describes someone who believes in the soon coming (or advent) of Jesus. Most Christians could probably describe themselves as an "adventist," because nearly all denominations teach that Jesus will in fact come again. Several times in the book of Revelation Christ said, "I am coming quickly!" (Revelation 3:11; see also Revelation 22:7, 12, 20). He also told His disciples, "I go to prepare a place for you. And if I go and prepare a place for you, I will come again" (John 14:2, 3).

The disciples and apostles spoke often of Christ's soon return and the shortness of life. They encouraged people to get ready for the imminent coming of Jesus. While nobody knows the exact date of Jesus' return, Bible prophecies do give us signs so we can know that His coming is near. Adventists believe God is preparing a people for this momentous event and that the Lord raised up a movement in this last generation—the age of Laodicea spoken of in Revelation 3:14–22—to help the world get ready for the advent of Jesus. Seventh-day Adventists look forward to Jesus' promised return just as a bride awaits the coming of her bridegroom.

---

11   http://www.gordonconwell.edu/resources/documents/StatusOfGlobalMission.pdf

THE ULTIMATE SACRIFICE

D esmond Doss put his life at risk on Guam, on Leyte in the Philippines, and on Okinawa in Japan, all in order to save others. His self-sacrificing acts of heroism were not intended to lift himself up, but were done because of his compassion toward his comrades. He even attempted to treat enemy soldiers in an effort to bring healing and comfort to all. While an imperfect man, his life reflected Jesus, who, to use the military term, paid the "supreme price" to save humanity from eternal death.

Seventh-day Adventists believe that Jesus Christ lived a perfect, sinless life in obedience to God's will. Through His life, death, and resurrection, He provided the means of saving people. His sacrifice paid the penalty of death, and everyone who accepts by faith His ultimate sacrifice may have eternal life. The gift of salvation cannot be earned through good works. It is freely offered to all people, regardless of race, gender, or social background.

The Adventists believe the Bible is a history of how deeply concerned heaven is for the salvation of the human race. The Father, Son, and Holy Spirit work together to bring lost people back into harmony with the Creator. The love of God for our world is most clearly expressed in the famous Bible verse that says, "God so loved the world that He gave His only begotten Son, that whoever believes in Him should not perish but have everlasting life" (John 3:16).

The devil portrays God as angry with people all the time, wanting to punish them for their sins. But the Bible reveals a God who loved lost humans so much that He willingly gave up His Son to save us. Such a sacrifice can hardly be understood, yet it is this love that moves our hearts to want to humbly give ourselves to the Lord. Seeing Jesus suffering on the cross for our sins causes us to see our own weaknesses and selfishness and to desire to be more like Him.

Adventists believe that when we give ourselves to the Lord in faith, we are adopted as sons and daughters of God. When we humbly confess our sins and express our desire to turn away from our self-centered way of living, the Holy Spirit comes into our hearts and begins to write God's law of love in our minds. We become transformed and are given power to live pure lives. This change of life continues as we daily abide in Jesus, and it gives us the assurance that we are saved now and until the final day of judgment.

One of the many myths about Seventh-day Adventists is that they believe they are the only ones who will be saved. That's not true. Quite the contrary, Adventists believe that the majority of God's followers are actually scattered among other denominations and faiths! There are many true Christians in other churches who may not fully understand everything taught in the Bible, but their hearts are right with God (see John 10:16). Godly people who love the Lord are found in many churches. There are also people with very little knowledge of God who, to the best of their ability, are following what they know to be right. They may have never even heard the name of Jesus but will be in the kingdom of heaven (see Romans 1:18–20).

Adventists also believe that as the last events of earth's history unfold and the warfare of Satan against God's people becomes more acute, that a clear knowledge of truth will be held up before the world and that those who truly want to follow the Lord will leave any church, religious belief, or organization that is opposed to the Bible (Revelation 18:4) and faithfully join those who "keep the commandments of God and the faith of Jesus" (Revelation 14:12).

Baptism

Seventh-day Adventists believe in following Jesus' example in baptism by immersion. The meaning of the New Testament word for *baptize* is to "dip or immerse," not sprinkle, as is seen in many Christian churches around the world.

This sacred act, which seals our love relationship with Christ, symbolizes three significant events in the life of a true believer: (1) death to sin, (2) birth to a new life in Christ, and (3) marriage to Christ for eternity. This spiritual union will grow stronger and sweeter with time, as long as love continues to grow.

When Christ was a young man, He was baptized by John the Baptist in the Jordan (see Matthew 3:13–15). When Jesus finished His ministry on earth, He told His disciples: "Go therefore and make disciples of all the nations, baptizing them in the name of the Father and of the Son and of the Holy Spirit" (Matthew 28:19). He also taught, "He who believes and is baptized will be saved; but he who does not believe will be condemned" (Mark 16:16).

The Seventh-day Adventist Church is not the only denomination that believes in baptism by immersion. Baptists, United Pentecostals, Anabaptists, and the Disciples of Christ also hold to this teaching. Biblical archaeologists have even uncovered depictions in the early church of baptism by immersion in water. [12]

The Lord's Supper

Like many Christian churches, Seventh-day Adventists celebrate the Lord's Supper, also called the Communion service, with unleavened bread and unfermented grape juice. When Christ celebrated the Passover with His disciples, He gave us the Lord's Supper to replace the Passover feast. Since leaven symbolized sin, unleavened bread and unfermented grape juice represented the pure and unpolluted life of Jesus.

The service is usually practiced four times a year in the Adventist Church, and begins uniquely with a foot-washing service after the manner of Jesus who washed His disciples' feet. The Bible says Jesus, "rose from supper and laid aside His garments, took a towel and girded Himself. After that, He poured water into a basin and began to wash the disciples' feet, and to wipe them with the towel with which He was girded" (John 13:4, 5).

The Adventists practice this service to help prepare one's heart for what is to follow. Christ, after He finished washing His disciples' feet, said, "If I then, your Lord and Teacher, have washed your feet, you also ought to wash one another's feet. For I have given you an example, that you should do as I have done to you" (verses 14, 15).

Taking part in the Lord's Supper by eating a small piece of unleavened bread and drinking a small amount of unfermented grape juice symbolizes one's acceptance of the body and blood of Jesus, broken and spilled for humanity. Taking these emblems represents our faith in what Christ has done for us. The service is intended to strengthen one's trust in Jesus and unite our hearts with other believers. When this special service is held in the Seventh-day Adventist Church, it is not limited to Adventists but is open to all believing Christians.

---

12   See https://en.wikipedia.org/wiki/Immersion_baptism

The Lord's Supper is done "in remembrance" of the ultimate sacrifice of Christ for each of us. The service is a time for careful reflection, yet filled with joy as participants contemplate the death of Jesus to save our world from a deadly enemy attack by Satan. Jesus did not risk His life on the battlefield of earth; He freely gave His life so that we might be saved.

HOPE IN TROUBLED TIMES

World War II must have felt and looked like the end of the world for the soldiers engaged in bloody battles in the European and Pacific theaters. Surrounded by bone-jarring bombings, chattering machine-gun fire, and cries from comrades dying all around them, these traumatic experiences etched images of horror into their minds forever. For the sixty million people who perished during the Second World War, it was their "last days."

Seventh-day Adventists believe that even more troubling times are ahead. They are confident that we are living in the final days of earth's history.

The Bible provides many signs that show we are nearing the soon return of Jesus. One of the indicators given by Christ is that, "Nation will rise against nation, and kingdom against kingdom" (Luke 21:10). Although many wars have marred history, never have they been so global and catastrophic. World Wars I and II caused more deaths and suffering than all previous wars put together. Pope Francis has said he believes World War III is beginning now in pieces through the recent surge of terrorists attacks experienced around the world.

Despite all the evil and pain we witness in these difficult days, Adventists look forward to the hope of Jesus' soon return. They believe God will carry them through a time of tribulation and then take them to heaven when Christ comes back to this earth. It will be a fearful day for those who reject Him, but a glorious day for those who have put their trust in God. Like Desmond, Adventists believe in God's promise, "He shall call upon Me, and I will answer him; I will be with him in trouble; I will deliver him and honor him" (Psalm 91:15).

The End of the World

Seventh-day Adventists take Jesus' predictions about the end of the age literally. In Matthew 24 (also Mark 13 and Luke 21), Christ's disciples asked Him, "What will be the sign of Your coming, and of the end of the age" (Matthew 24:3). Jesus provided a host of predictions to let His followers know when His coming is near. But He never gave an exact date. "Of that day and hour no one knows, not even the angels of heaven, but My Father only" (verse 36).

A myth about Seventh-day Adventists is that they have predicted the day of Christ's return. This is simply untrue; the church has never made such a prediction. William Miller, who was a Baptist, predicted that Jesus would come back in 1844, but the Adventist Church wasn't around then. It was formally established in 1863—almost twenty years later.

The Bible reveals many different types of signs that let us know that the end of the world is imminent. Some indicators can be seen in the natural world, with an increase in earthquakes and other disasters. Others are revealed in the religious world, including a great religious awakening and, at the same time, a decline in religious interest. The dramatic increase in worldwide missions, the translation of the Bible into many languages, and the good news of Christ's return going around the world, are all signs that Jesus will soon return. Sadly, other signs point to an increase of evil, murder, crime, immorality, wars, famines, and religious persecution.

The Coming of Christ

Seventh-day Adventists believe Christ's return will be literal, personal, visible, and worldwide. Desmond believed that when Jesus comes, the righteous dead will be resurrected and, along with the righteous living, be glorified with new bodies and caught up to heaven, but the unrighteous will die.

Adventists also believe in the certainty of Jesus' return. Christ said, "I will come again" (John 14:3). While the Bible predicts false christs and false prophets would appear, Jesus will come "in like manner" as He left (Acts 1:11). The same personal Savior will return as a real, tangible being—not some spirit entity.

The Bible also says His return will be visible: "He is coming with clouds, and every eye will see Him" (Revelation 1:7), and that His coming will be audible, with "a great sound of a trumpet" (Matthew 24:31). The event will be cataclysmic. No human kingdom will exist after Jesus returns.

While Christians will be aware of the nearness of Jesus' coming, most of the world will be caught off guard. The Bible says, "You yourselves know perfectly that the day of the Lord so comes as a thief in the night" (1 Thessalonians 5:2). Jesus said, "You also be ready, for the Son of Man is coming at an hour you do not expect" (Matthew 24:44).

Some take this comparison to a thief to mean that Christ's return will be in secret, but the apostle Paul's point is that, for the worldly minded, His coming will be as unexpected as that of a thief. Seventh-day Adventists do not believe in the teaching of the "secret rapture" as popularized by the *Left Behind* films. While they believe God's people will be taken up, they also believe, based on the Bible, that the coming of Jesus will be anything but a secret.

The Millennium

The book of Revelation provides insights into the events preceding the coming of Jesus as well as what happens after His return. Seventh-day Adventists believe that after Christ comes there will be a thousand-year period when God's people will live and reign with Jesus in heaven. This "millennium" (which is a term not found in the Bible, but simply means 1,000 years) will be a time when the wicked dead will be judged and the earth will be desolate. In accordance with the Bible, Adventists are premillennialists; that is, they believe Jesus comes *before* the millennium begins.

At the end of the thousand years, the wicked will be raised from the dead, the final judgment will take place, and then all the wicked, along with Satan and his evil angels, will be destroyed in the lake of fire. This punishment will completely burn them up. Nothing will be left, according to the Bible, except ashes (see Malachi 4:1–3). The universe will be free of evil and sin forever.

The Earth Made New

When the earth has been cleansed by fire of all sin, Seventh-day Adventists believe this earth will be made new and restored to its state before sin entered our world. (Desmond was certainly looking forward to this event!) The new earth will be a real place where the righteous will dwell with God. It will be the eternal home of the redeemed and contain a perfect environment without sickness, hatred, or natural disasters. All suffering and death will be gone and the Lord Himself will live with His people. The pain and loss of the past will be forgotten, for God will wipe away all tears (Revelation 21:4).

The capital city of the new earth will be called the New Jerusalem. The city is beautiful and described as "a bride adorned for her husband" (Revelation 21:2). God's glory illuminates the city. It is made of most precious stones and gold so pure that it is "like clear glass" (verse 18). From out of the throne in the center of the city flows a river of water of life with the Tree of Life growing on both sides of the river. The redeemed will partake of the fruit of this tree and live forever.

Most of all, Seventh-day Adventists believe that when the earth is made new, the great battle between good and evil will be forever ended. No more fighting, killing, or wars. Sin and sinners are gone and troubled times will never again invade our world. The whole universe will be clean and the harmonious power of God will be known everywhere. From the smallest particle to the largest galaxy, all creation will declare that God is love.

PREPARE TO MEET YOUR MAKER

D esmond was acutely aware of death and how vulnerable he was in combat without a weapon. Therefore, he tried to be always ready to meet his Maker. Indeed, none of us is immune to the grim reaper. Death eventually knocks at the door of every human being.

But what happens when we die? Do we immediately go to heaven or hell or some temporary place in between? When we breathe our last, do we simply turn back into dirt? Is there life after death? Let's briefly look at the beliefs of Desmond and the Seventh-day Adventists about the state of the dead, as well as the Bible's teaching on hell.

What Happens at Death

One teaching that Adventists interpret very differently than do other Christians, is what happens when a person dies. Seventh-day Adventists believe that at death, we enter into a state of unconsciousness until the resurrection. Jesus repeatedly referred to this state by using the word "sleep" (see John 11:11–14). The Bible teaches that death is a dreamless, peaceful type of rest until one of two resurrections.

Some people use 2 Corinthians 5:8 to teach that when we are absent from the body we are present with the Lord; a Christian's spirit goes straight to heaven at death, and then their spirit and body are reunited at Jesus' second coming. While many people believe this view, Adventists do not believe it is based in the Bible.

It is true that to be absent from the body is to be present with the Lord. If you are saved and you die, your next conscious thought will be at the resurrection when you will be raised and see Jesus. Scripture explains that the "dead know nothing" (Ecclesiastes 9:5), so you have no consciousness when you are in the grave.

When Jesus told Martha, "[Lazarus] will rise again" (John 11:23), she replied, "I know that he will rise again in the resurrection at the last day" (verse 24). She did not believe he was already alive, and she understood that the resurrection would happen "at the last day." That time has not yet come.

Many of the Protestant reformers believed that when people die, they sleep in the grave until the resurrection morning when Jesus returns. It was the mythological teachings of the Dark Ages that led many to believe in an immortal soul that could never die. Notice this quote from Martin Luther found in *The Christian Hope,* by Dr. T. A. Kantonen, on page 35: "For just as one who falls asleep and reaches morning unexpectedly when he awakes, without knowing what has happened to him, we shall suddenly rise on the last day without knowing how we have come into death and through death."

William Tyndale also believed that the soul is mortal and that when one dies, he is unconscious, asleep in the grave until Jesus' return. Many of the great reformers believed in the Seventh-day Adventist interpretation of the state of the dead.

Since "the wages of sin is death" (Romans 6:23) and "all have sinned and fall short of the glory of God" (Romans 3:23), all people are subject to death. The last enemy to be destroyed is death. Paul explained, "For as in Adam all die, even so in Christ all shall be made alive" (1 Corinthians 15:22). And when will we be made alive? Paul answered, "Afterward those who are Christ's *at His coming*" (verse 23, emphasis added).

The Bible presents about twelve stories of people being resurrected, stories that demonstrate God's power to raise people at the coming of Christ. In not one case does the person make a comment about knowing anything while dead. You would think the very first question these people would be asked is, "What was it like to be dead? What did you experience?" The Bible record is silent because the Scriptures teach that when a person dies, his plans perish (see Psalm 146:3, 4).

Hell

Seventh-day Adventists have been accused of not believing in hell. In fact, not only do Adventists believe the lost will burn in hell, but in one sense, their hell is hotter than what most Southern Baptists believe. Baptists believe in a hell that simmers sinners forever, but Adventists believe the fires of hell are so hot that they actually burn up the wicked. They believe the Bible does not teach that sinners are eternally tortured in hell.

During the Dark Ages, it was very profitable for the church to scare people with the idea that the wicked will be tormented forever. Some still teach that as soon as a wicked person dies, even before a judgment, that person immediately goes to hell to burn eternally for the sins of one lifetime. Even if he has lived only twenty years, he will burn for billions and billions … and billions of years. Jesus did not teach this view. Christ said we have two choices: Believe and live or do not believe and perish (see John 3:16). The dictionary defines "perish" as: "To die or be killed; to cease to exist." [13]

Adventists, like Desmond, point to the devil's first lie to Eve in the Garden of Eden: "You will *not* surely die" (Genesis 3:4, emphasis added) and conclude that the doctrine of burning forever comes from Satan. God told Adam and Eve that "in the day that you eat of it [the tree of the knowledge of good and evil] you shall surely die" (Genesis 2:17). The unbiblical view of an immortal soul leads to the equally unbiblical belief of an eternally burning hell.

Someday, when Jesus comes, those who believe in Him will "put on immortality" (1 Corinthians 15:53). The righteous receive the gift of eternal life at the resurrection. At the last judgment the wicked will be cast into hell along with Satan and his evil angels. Another term used for hell in the Bible is "the lake of fire" and is described as "the second death" in which death itself is forever destroyed (Revelation 20:14). The Bible says that the fire will "burn them up" (Malachi 4:1), that fire will come "down from God out of heaven," and that the wicked will be "devoured" (Revelation 20:9).

Seventh-day Adventists do not hold a monopoly on the teaching that the fires of hell will do their work of destroying sin and then go out. This was the view of John Stott, one of the most influential evangelical theologians of our time. Many Christian leaders from various denominations have shared "off the record" that they are in agreement with Adventists on the subject of hell. More and more leading scholars have come to recognize that the idea of God eternally tormenting sinners is nothing more than distorted medieval theology that crept into many churches. [14]

When Desmond told his comrade that he should be prepared to meet his Maker, he didn't mean that he would instantly stand before the judgment throne of God or immediately be sent to heaven or hell. He meant that when he died he would have forever sealed his decision for or against

---

13   http://www.merriam-webster.com/dictionary/perish

14   See Edward William Fudge, *The Fire That Consumes: A Biblical and Historical Study of the Doctrine of Final Punishment* (Eugene, OR: Wipf and Stock Publishers, 2011).

the Lord. There is no second chance after death. We enter the grave with our choice in place, and that decision will stand forever.

The teaching of an eternally burning hellfire that torments sinners forever—even if they have only lived a short lifetime—presents a sadistic picture of God. Revelation tells us that following the judgment there will be no more sorrow, pain, or tears (Revelation 21:4). The Bible also tells of Jesus coming to suffer death on the cross and paying the penalty for our sins to save us. God is not looking for ways to keep people out of heaven and send them to a place of eternal torment; He has done everything possible to open the gates of heaven and invite us in.

FOLLOWING ORDERS

As a child, Desmond was fascinated by a small, framed picture of the Ten Commandments hanging on the wall of his parent's living room. When they were gone he would pull up a chair and stand on it to get a closer look. He was taught that these ten rules from heaven were not to be ignored. Loyalty to one of these commandments was severely tested while Doss served in the military—"Remember the Sabbath day, to keep it holy" (Exodus 20:8). When God's laws and the commands of his officers were in conflict, Desmond's custom was to obey "higher orders."

Seventh-day Adventists have been labeled by some as legalists because of their belief in the eternal nature of God's law. But building upon the foundation of the Bible, they believe that the Decalogue was not done away with, but stands as an eternal expression of God's love, will, and purpose for our lives. In the heart of the Ten Commandments is the fourth commandment, to remember the Sabbath. Do people who seek to follow God's laws do so only as an attempt to earn their salvation?

God's Law of Love

Another myth about Seventh-day Adventists is that they believe they will be saved by keeping the law. The Bible clearly states: "By grace you have been saved through faith, and that not of yourselves; it is the gift of God, not of works, lest anyone should boast" (Ephesians 2:8, 9). Adventists teach that salvation is all grace and not of works.

Salvation can never come by our efforts to keep the Ten Commandments. We can never hope to gain entrance into the kingdom of heaven by not lying, not stealing, or by keeping the Sabbath. None of our works can atone for our sins. Adventists believe that, "In infinite love and mercy God made Christ, who knew no sin, to be sin for us, so that in Him we might be made the righteousness of God." [15]

---

15   https://www.adventist.org/en/beliefs/salvation/the-experience-of-salvation/

Because Seventh-day Adventists believe that the Ten Commandments were not done away with, people may confuse their emphasis on the importance of the law to mean that we are saved by keeping the law. The truth is that people are saved by grace and that the fruit of true faith leads to obedience through the power of the Holy Spirit.

Adventists do not keep the law in order to be saved, but because they are saved. People can be saved only by grace through faith, and the fruit of genuine faith is obedience. Jesus once said, "If you love Me, keep My commandments" (John 14:15). Notice what comes first in this Bible verse: "If you love Me ...." Love is the motivating factor in keeping God's commandments, not the attempt to be saved.

Jesus said to "keep My commandments." He didn't say to keep 50 percent or 80 percent of them, but to keep all of them. John wrote: "He who says, 'I know Him,' and does not keep His commandments, is a liar, and the truth is not in him" (1 John 2:4).

While many have a negative view toward God's law because it points out sin in their lives, Adventists see the law as a way to bring them to Christ. Paul said, "The law is holy, and the commandment holy and just and good" (Romans 7:12). He added that "by the law is the knowledge of sin" (3:20). Seventh-day Adventists do not see the law as restrictive, but as something that gives freedom. "He who looks into the perfect law of liberty and continues in it, and is not a forgetful hearer but a doer of the work, this one will be blessed in what he does" (James 1:25).

Desmond did not like to be called a "conscientious objector," but rather, a "conscientious cooperator." He wanted the draft board to know that he was more than willing to defend his country. When his draft letter finally came, his employer in the shipyard where he worked offered to try to get him excused from serving, but he didn't go along with that.

In a similar way, Seventh-day Adventists are not looking for ways to avoid serving God. They feel a loyalty to the Lord and seek to keep the commandments from a heart of love. They understand that it is impossible to obey God without the power of the Holy Spirit. But when Jesus is invited to live within, the result is a change of attitude toward the law. They agree with King David: "I delight to do Your will, O my God, and Your law is within my heart" (Psalm 40:8).

A Sign of Loyalty

In the center of God's law is the fourth commandment that says, "Remember the Sabbath day, to keep it holy. Six days you shall labor and do all your work, but the seventh day is the Sabbath of the LORD your God" (Exodus 20:8–10). Is this a relic of the old covenant, a command applying only to the Jews, or a law that was modified during the time of Christ?

Well, Desmond believed that the Sabbath was established at the creation of the world, long before there were any Jews, and that its blessing was intended for all humanity. After the six days of Creation were completed, the Bible says, "Thus the heavens and the earth, and all the host of them, were finished. And on the seventh day God ended His work which He had done, and He rested on the seventh day from all His work which He had done. Then God blessed the seventh day and sanctified it, because in it He rested from all His work which God had created and made" (Genesis 2:1–3).

To bless and sanctify a day means more than saying it's a nice day. God made the Sabbath holy. It is sacred time in the week to come before Him and acknowledge that He is our Creator and Redeemer.

The Sabbath was not established to be a burden to people. It was a gift from God to give us time for rest and restoration, for worship and fellowship, for a time to remember that we are not saved by our works but that we might rest in God's work done for us. When we keep the Sabbath, we demonstrate our loyalty to God just as a husband shows his loyalty to his wife. God said, "I also gave them My Sabbaths, to be a sign between them and Me, that they might know that I am the LORD who sanctifies them" (Ezekiel 20:12).

Adventists also believe that Satan, the enemy of humanity, wants to smear God's name and break people's loyalty to the Lord. They understand that there would be an attack on God's laws and there would be efforts to change the Sabbath. A power would rise up and "intend to change times and law" (Daniel 7:25). During the period after the early church, the established church began to compromise and slowly made this change from Saturday to Sunday.[16]

---

16 Desmond Doss explains this change in a conversation with another medic in *The Unlikeliest Hero*, pp. 34, 35.

And so, the one commandment most often forgotten is the fourth commandment—even though it begins, "*Remember* the Sabbath day, to keep it holy" (Exodus 20:8, emphasis added). Many have tried to set aside this command. It would seem odd that the one commandment that people attempt to forget is the only one God specifically said to remember.

Salvation does not come to anyone by keeping the commandments; rather, salvation leads us to keep all the commandments. We are not saved by keeping the seventh-day Sabbath any more than by not stealing or not committing adultery. Our motive for keeping the law is that we love God and want to keep His law.

Isaiah described the proper motive we should have toward the Sabbath and the blessings God will bring to those who do not desecrate it, in the same way we would avoid walking on our country's flag.

"If you turn away your foot from the Sabbath, from doing your pleasure on My holy day, and call the Sabbath a delight, the holy day of the LORD honorable, and shall honor Him, not doing your own ways, nor finding your own pleasure, nor speaking your own words, then you shall delight yourself in the LORD; and I will cause you to ride on the high hills of the earth, and feed you with the heritage of Jacob your father. The mouth of the LORD has spoken" (Isaiah 58:13, 14).

Like Desmond, who once held up an entire army on Sabbath so that he could worship the Lord and pray, Adventists consider it a privilege to keep the Sabbath holy, for this day is not a bothersome command, but a day of delight.

HEALING AND SAVING LIVES

A common misconception people have about Seventh-day Adventists is that they do not believe in blood transfusions. Actually, Adventists are known worldwide for their emphasis on health and healing. Indeed, their extensive medical work and disaster relief programs are found on every continent.

Desmond demonstrated by his own personal example as a boy (when he happily donated blood for a transfusion) and as an adult that a Seventh-day Adventist follows the example of Jesus by having compassion toward the suffering.

A Ministry of Healing

One of the most well-known activities of Seventh-day Adventists is bringing healing to others. Jesus taught, "You shall love the LORD your God with all your heart … and your neighbor as yourself" (Luke 10:27). The Bible spends more time on Jesus' ministering to the sick and suffering than on His preaching and teaching. Sometimes Jesus would pass through villages and heal every hurting person in the entire town.

In the last couple of years, you may have seen Seventh-day Adventists in the news providing free medical treatment to large numbers of people in places like Oakland, San Francisco, and Spokane. On April 8–10, 2015, over 6,000 community people received help in the Alamodome in San Antonio. In April 2016, over 10,000 people lined up to receive more than $30 million worth of free healthcare in Los Angeles in just two and a half days. Besides doing surgeries, the clinic also gave out free clothing, free legal services, haircuts, and tattoo-removal services—all on a volunteer basis.

The love of Jesus was shared through more than just free medical clinics in large cities in the United States. Christ's example of service has led the Adventist Church to create a worldwide community service program called Adventist Development and Relief Agency (ADRA). This global humanitarian organization demonstrates God's love and compassion by bringing emergency relief to people in poverty and distress in more than

130 countries. ADRA works with many different types of programs such as hunger and nutrition, disaster relief, clean water and sanitation, children, and economic relief.

Healthcare ministry is another way Desmond's church shows God's love. Worldwide, there are over 170 Seventh-day Adventist hospitals that bring healing to the sick and suffering. There are also 140 nursing homes and retirement centers, 385 clinics and dispensaries, twenty-nine orphanages and children's homes, and seven airplanes and medical launches. All of these annually serve over 18.5 million outpatient visits. [17] In the United States, nearly 120,000 employees serve about ten million people a year in eighty-four hospitals, urgent-care clinics, home-health agencies, long-term care facilities, and hospices. [18]

Healthy Living

Because the Bible teaches "that your body is the temple of the Holy Spirit" and that you should "glorify God in your body" (1 Corinthians 6:19, 20), Seventh-day Adventists practice healthful living. This includes more than just the physical body. Their beliefs state: "We are called to be a godly people who think, feel, and act in harmony with biblical principles in all aspects of personal and social life. For the Spirit to recreate in us the character of our Lord we involve ourselves only in those things that will produce Christlike purity, health, and joy in our lives." [19]

Because of an emphasis on caring for one's health, a number of studies have shown that Adventists live an average of ten years longer than the average citizen. In November 2005, Dan Buettner wrote for *National Geographic* magazine, "The Secrets of Long Life." He uncovered places in the world where people live longer and called them "blue zones." One blue zone is Loma Linda, California—not because of geography, but because it has a high population of Adventists. Buettner studied their lifestyle practices—things like eating a vegetarian diet, exercising, drinking plenty of water—and learned that one thing Adventists do that contributes to their health is keeping the Sabbath. Taking a weekly break from the daily rigors

---

17 https://www.adventistarchives.org/quick-statistics-on-the-seventh-day-adventist-church

18 http://www.sdahealthcare.org/

19 https://www.adventist.org/en/beliefs/living/christian-behavior/

of life to focus on God, family, and friends relieves stress and strengthens social bonds.

A simple acronym captures the principles of healthy living practiced by Seventh-day Adventists—NEWSTART. These eight letters outline eight laws of health that bring energy, peace, and joy to the Adventists who practice them. They are proper Nutrition, regular Exercise, an adequate amount of pure Water, a healthy amount of Sunlight, moderation through Temperance (abstaining from alcohol, tobacco, narcotics, and recreational drugs), fresh Air, adequate Rest, and a Trust in God's power. [20]

Seventh-day Adventists also believe that our amusements and entertainment should reach the highest standards of taste and beauty. Even how we dress—in modesty and simplicity—speaks of our relationship with God and impacts our health and associations. Adventists discourage excessive adornment and believe God values most the beauty of character.

In a conversation with a fellow soldier, Desmond was once asked why he didn't smoke cigarettes or occasionally drink whiskey. After sharing that the apostle Paul said our bodies are the temple of the Holy Spirit, Desmond explained, "That's what we go on, that the body is the temple of God, and we won't defile the temple with nicotine or alcohol or even coffee or tea. I don't think I'm missing much there, either. I used to smoke corn silk cigarettes when I was a kid, and sometimes a cigarette butt, but all they did was make me cough."

Desmond wondered, "How could he explain to this happy-go-lucky buddy of his that, even if the abstinences did seem harsh, the positive attributes of Adventism made such minor sacrifices worthwhile? He was no gloomy Gus; Adventists are a happy group of people." [21]

---

20   http://newstart.com/what-is-newstart1/#sthash.PBPqz4QL.dpbs

21   *The Unlikeliest Hero*, p. 37.

A FINAL VERDICT

D esmond was considered an oddball, a headache, and a troublemaker by his officers. There was strong prejudice against conscientious objectors, nicknamed "conchies," because they were often seen as slackers looking for a way to get out of the military.

"You guys are all alike," one of his sergeants accused him. "You talk big about religious freedom, but when your country needs you to help protect that freedom you chicken out."

Desmond replied, "That's where you're wrong, sergeant."[22] The heroic actions of Doss confirmed his words.

Some people have wrong ideas about the Seventh-day Adventist Church. They have read misinformation or heard others label them a cult. This kind of prejudice has kept some from objectively looking at the teachings of this church.

The apostle Paul was once accused of being the instigator of a questionable sect. Prejudiced religious leaders bitterly stated, "We have found this man a plague, a creator of dissension among all the Jews throughout the world, and a ringleader of the sect of the Nazarenes" (Acts 24:5). He was basically accused of being the leader of a cult!

Yet notice how simply this follower of Jesus explained his beliefs. "This I confess to you, that according to the Way which they call a sect, so I worship the God of my fathers, believing all things which are written in the Law and in the Prophets" (verse 14).

Seventh-day Adventists are often called "people of the book" because of their insistence in standing on the rock of Scripture. When confronted by deep questions, difficult trials, and misunderstandings about their teachings, they are quick to ask, "What does the Bible say?"

The Word of God predicts that a time is coming to our earth that will shake the strongest beliefs of every person on the planet. Traumatic world events and maddening political movements will drive people to dig into

---

22   Ibid., p. 21, 22.

their Bibles as never before. Like Desmond, many Christians will stand before leaders to testify for their faith. Their words will not fall on deaf ears.

What do you believe about our world, about the vexing times in which we live, about the deterioration of society and the catastrophic disasters unleashed in the natural world? Jesus gave us advice for surviving the most tumultuous storms ever poured over humanity.

"Whoever hears these sayings of Mine, and does them, I will liken him to a wise man who built his house on the rock: and the rain descended, the floods came, and the winds blew and beat on that house; and it did not fall, for it was founded on the rock" (Matthew 7:24, 25).

THERE'S **MORE** TO THIS **STORY!**

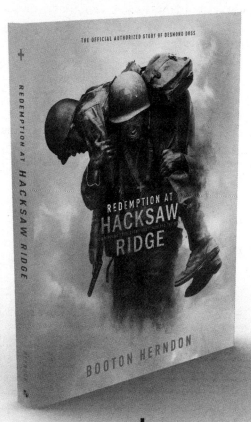

✝

REDEMPTION AT
HACKSAW
THE GRIPPING TRUE STORY THAT INSPIRED THE MOVIE
RIDGE

Get your copy of the expanded hardcover edition today!

This beautiful hardcover release has nearly 100 pages of extra content. Journey deeper into the story of Desmond Doss and learn even more of this inspirational story. Includes actual photos and many more great features.

Visit www.remnantpublications.com or call (800) 423-1319 for more information.